IMAGES
of Sport

NEWPORT RUGBY
FOOTBALL CLUB
1950-2000

This Newport team defeated Harlequins 21-0 at Twickenham on 18 December 1954. From left to right, back row: G. Keeley, J. Lane, I. Ford, G. Price, G. Morris, J. Hancock, R. Carter (linesman). Middle row: B. Meredith, D. Ackerman, M. Thomas (captain), K. Jones, H. Morgan, G. Whitson. Front row: D.O. Brace, R. Burnett, G. Owen.

IMAGES
of Sport

NEWPORT RUGBY FOOTBALL CLUB 1950-2000

Compiled by
Steve Lewis

TEMPUS

First published 2000
Copyright © Steve Lewis, 2000

Tempus Publishing Limited
The Mill, Brimscombe Port,
Stroud, Gloucestershire, GL5 2QG

ISBN 0 7524 2084 4

Typesetting and origination by
Tempus Publishing Limited
Printed in Great Britain by
Midway Clark Printing, Wiltshire

Also available from Tempus Publishing

Blackheath RFC	Dave Hammomd	0 7524 1688 X
Bristol RFC	Mark Hoskins/Dave Fox	0 7524 1875 0
Cardiff RFC	Duncan Gardiner/Alan Evans	0 7524 1608 1
The Five Nations Story	David Hands	0 7524 1851 3
Llanelli RFC	Bob Harragan	0 7524 1134 9
Newcastle RFC	Alan Hedley	0 7524 2046 1
Newport RFC: 1874-1950	Steve Lewis	0 7524 1570 0
Newport County FC	Richard Shepherd	0 7524 1081 4
Swansea Town FC	Richard Shepherd	0 7524 1133 0
Glamorgan CCC	Andrew Hignell	0 7524 0792 9
Glamorgan CCC 2	Andrew Hignell	0 7524 1137 3
Glamorgan CCC 100 Greats	Andrew Hignell	0 7524 1879 3

Contents

Acknowledgements

In compiling this book I was fortunate to receive encouragement and help from many sources. It is appropriate to take the opportunity to thank those concerned as the book would not have been completed without them.

Material was supplied by Doug Ackerman, John Billot, Brian Cresswell, Keith Clarke, R.T. Evans, Keith Jarrett, Gordon Keeley, Rhys Morgan, Alf Panting, David Rogers, Peter Smith, Jeff Watkins, David Watkins and Keith Wigmore. In addition, photographers Phil Bird (David Waters portrait) and Steve Hoggetts (Newport team photograph 1999/2000) were generous in allowing the inclusion of their work.

The staff at Newport Reference Library, Kevin Ward (Deputy Editor) and Steve Phillips (Photograph Editor) at the *South Wales Argus*, the Welsh Rugby Union and all the administration staff at Newport Rugby Football Club – particularly Mrs Jean Evans who fielded all my queries very capably and ensured that all my requests were accommodated0.

The support of James Howarth at Tempus Publishing Ltd in believing that Newport RFC should be the subject of two books covering its 125-year history is appreciated and I hope the books meet with his expectations. Finally, my wife Catherine whose constant cajoling, nudging, kicking and so on, which ensured that this book was delivered only three months late. She also typed it, correcting where necessary, but I must take sole responsibility for any inaccuracies in the text. While every effort has been made to contact copyright holders of the material used, any party wishing to pursue this matter should contact me through Tempus Publishing Ltd.

Foreword

I was first introduced to the game of rugby on 11 January 1961. The occasion was the visit of the South African tourists to Rodney Parade. Schools were given a half day off to enable pupils, and presumably teachers, to have the chance to go to the match. These games against the major touring sides were big events in the town's calendar and it is a particularly sad that such days are now a thing of the past.

My father was not interested in any sport and, looking back, I find it hard to explain why he decided to take me to the game. To the best of my knowledge it was the only rugby game he ever attended but, sadly, he is no longer around to clarify the issue. I would be lying if I said that I had vivid recollections of the day. The records show that the result, a 3-0 win for the visitors, but to pretend that I knew what was going on, or indeed why, would not hold water. What I do know with the utmost certainty however, is that I liked what I saw and wanted more.

Almost forty years later I could not begin to estimate the number of games of rugby I have seen. I love it. I love my side winning, I have a certain masochistic tolerance of the inevitable defeats but I have never, and never will, enjoy a drawn game: I come away feeling short-changed, totally unsatisfied and almost wishing the game had been lost.

My first season ticket was for 1962/63 and, for the princely sum of £1, it allowed me admittance to the ground for all home games excepting matches against touring sides. Just right of halfway in the enclosure was the favoured spot and for the next ten years, if Newport were at home, this is where I would be. A great autograph hunter during the period, I am sure I could have papered my walls with David Watkins' signature. Some of my fondest memories are of David dancing over the hallowed turf avoiding the clutches of of opposing back row forwards. The 19 October 1967 was a sad day indeed when those b******s up north snatched our hero.

I remember one game when Newport were beaten by a couple of points. Gwynn Walters was the referee and, running onto the pitch at the end of the match, I was taught a salutary lesson that holds good to this day. Walters had denied Newport a 'try' and in my enthusiasm I apporoched the great man and asked – 'Why didn't you give that try, Ref?'. Walters looked me up and down for a moment and then said – 'If I didn't give it, lad, it wasn't a try'. Even in this age of TV cameras everywhere except up the players' backsides the comment is still relevant.

The 1970s saw the Centenary season, cup success and boys I played with at school (at rugby that is) win Welsh caps and, indeed, become British Lions. It has always fascinated me, this ageing process. When you are younger than the players they all look old. Then you go through a period of consolidation of ages and yet they still all look older than you. Then, ten or twenty years later, you look at the players and, yes, they all look older than you! I know that I'm deluding myself but I just cannot accept the fact that I am twenty years older than the most senior member of the Newport team. Am I alone in this?

During this period I made the move upstairs and now watch home matches from the dubious comfort of seat BE6. In addition to the discomfort of watching Newport struggle through the 1990s is the required position one has to adopt in the seats from the old national stadium that were installed in the stand at Rodney Parade. The experience will no doubt be of benefit, however, on away trips to France when crouching skills are required for the completion of natural bodily functions.

This volume ends in South Africa. On 3 June 2000, when Newport took the field at Kings Park, Durban (the ABSA Stadium as it is now known) to play the Natal Sharks. After almost forty years of following the Black and Ambers it was a particularly proud moment to witness the rejuvenated team compete in front of 34,000 spectators in one of the world's greatest stadiums. This was indeed a fitting finale to 125 years of Newport rugby.

In compiling this book and its predecessor certain parameters had to be observed. I had 240 pages to work with – room for approximately 400 photographic items and and roughly 40,000 words. These restrictions inevitably meant that much would have to be excluded and apoogies are in order to those many players and officials whose contribution to the history of this fine club are not properly recognised in these two volumes.

It is appropriate that the opportunity is taken to correct errors that appeared in *Newport Rugby Football Club 1874-1950*. Firstly, Arthur Gould captained Wales 18 times, not 17 as suggested on page 33. Although spelt differently in reference works, Gallaher is the correct spelling of the All Black captain featured on page 48. John Phillips 'Jack' Jones played for Pontypool and Newport as featured on page 64, not John Arthur Jones. Finally, on page 85, W.J. Martin (football honorary secretary) has regrettably been cropped from the team photograph.

In conclusion, I hope readers get as much pleasure in reading this book as I had in compiling it. I could not have scripted a better ending. After 125 years of rugby the club is now right back at the top of the game in Wales. What's that old saying? The cream always rises – you'd better believe it!

Steve Lewis
Newport
August 2000

One
The Good Old Days

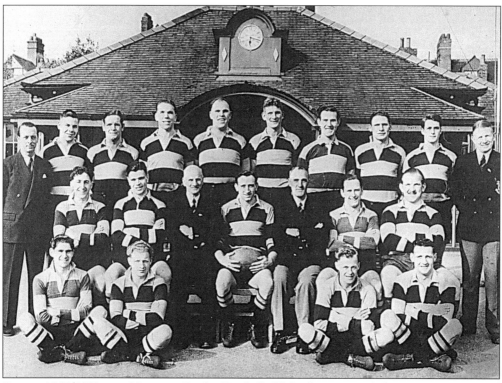

Season 1950/1951 saw Newport Rugby Football Club play some of the most exciting and entertaining rugby seen at Rodney Parade since the club's formation in 1874. Under the captaincy of Ken Jones the side won 37 of the 40 matches played. Two defeats were suffered, both away, at the hands of Harlequins and Exeter. At home Newport were also held to a 3-3 draw by Cardiff. It can be strongly argued that the two calendar years 1950 and 1951 represented the finest period in the club's 125-year history. Of 81 first team matches played, a total of 71 were won with 4 draws and 6 defeats. This First XV photograph for the 1950/1951 season shows, from left to right, back row: R. Lewis (hon. trainer), D.A.G. Ackerman, T. Sterry, L.E.T. Jones, B. Edwards, P. Davies, S. Kimpton, R. Hughes, J. Lane, R.T. Carter (match hon. secretary). Middle row: B. Williams, R.T. Evans (vice-captain), J.J. Wetter (chairman), K.J. Jones (captain), W.A. Everson (football hon. secretary), G. Ross, G.R. Hirst. Front row: R.D. Owen, R. Burnett, W.A. Williams, L. Davies.

The club's strength in depth at the start of the 1950s can be confirmed by the records of the United XV and the Extras. The United XV lost only 1 game of 28 played, scoring 425 points and conceding 54, while the Extras remained undefeated during the season. This picture shows the United XV in season 1950/1951. From left to right, back row: H. Brooks (trainer), D. Whelan, E. Nash, G. Keeley, H. Davies, I. Ford, G. Jenkins, M. Lewis, J. Blackborrow, H. Tovey, V. Parfitt (fixture hon. secretary). Middle row: R. Rowland, L. Smith, J.J. Wetter (chairman), J. Travers (captain), A. Panting (match hon. secretary), M. Everson, K. Sargeant. Front row: A.H. Rowland, J. Thomas.

On 24 February 1951, Blackheath were the visitors to Rodney Parade. In winning the game 20-8, Newport created a club record that stands to this day: this was their thirty-fifth consecutive win, a run of success which had started against Cardiff on 1 April 1950. In addition to Cardiff and Blackheath, clubs beaten included Swansea, Llanelli, Neath, Bath, Bristol, Leicester, Coventry and Gloucester. The programme notes advise that the following Saturday's home match against Cardiff would be all-ticket. A crowd of 27,000 saw Newport's run of victories end when the match ended in a 3-3 draw, with Cardiff also denying Newport the much sought-after four wins in a season. The Supporters' Club news page in the programme offered a coach trip to the Harlequins match on 17 March. Fans could also see the England versus Scotland international on the same day. Departing Friday night and returning Saturday, the price including all meals was 32/- (£1.60)!

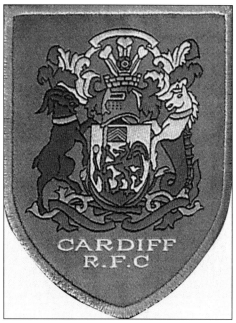

The crests of two of the most famous club sides in world rugby. The names Newport RFC and Cardiff RFC – founded in 1874 and 1876 respectively – are recognised wherever the game is played.

One week prior to the Blackheath game Newport visited Cardiff. Games between these greatest of rivals had become perhaps the most eagerly anticipated of the season by followers of both teams. Jack Davies in his definitive *One Hundred Years of Newport Rugby* wrote: 'I think the Cardiff-Newport match of 17 February 1951 deserves to rank as the outstanding club game of the century'. A world record attendance for a club match of over 48,000 saw Newport win by 8-3. This record attendance would only be broken at cup finals during the 1980s and 1990s. These programme pages show how the teams lined up. Note the advert for Gwyn Nicholls and Winfield Ltd. Almost fifty years earlier, Nicholls had joined Newport for a brief period when the business opened premises in the town.

Newport forwards hack the ball through a disputed line-out in this encounter played in November 1954. The club stockings help to identify the teams – Newport have two bands at the top while the top of the Cardiff stocking is one colour. Cardiff won this match 6-3. Huge crowds attended these local derbies and the old North Stand and terracing at Cardiff Arms Park are full to capacity.

Newport scrum-half Onllwyn Brace watches as the Cardiff forwards win a line-out during the 3-3 draw at Rodney Parade in March 1954. Number ten for Cardiff is Stan Bowes, one of the club's great servants who first played for the Arms Park side before the Second World War in the 1938/39 season.

Newport first met French opposition on 26 February 1900 when Stade Français were the visitors to Rodney Parade. A regular fixture with Racing Club de France was established in the 1920s, playing home and away in alternate seasons. Both Stade Français and Racing Club de France were Paris based clubs, but it was decided to travel to the south-west of the country over the New Year in 1951/52 and play two matches in Cognac and Nantes. Both games were won by – 6-5 and 8-3 respectively – but the tour proved to be very demanding. A round trip of 1,400 miles, rough sea crossings, lavish receptions and banquets would hardly seem appropriate preparation for the visit of the Fourth Springboks on 10 January. Shown here is a rare copy of the match programme for the Cognac match, which introduces Newport Athletic Club as 'The Number One British Side voted Club of the Year 1950 by the British Press'. The match was attended by a crowd of 6,000 spectators.

31 DÉCEMBRE
1951

PARC DES SPORTS
À 15 HEURES

Sous le patronage de

SUD-OUEST

GRAND MATCH INTERNATIONAL
DE RUGBY

NEWPORT ATHLETIC CLUB
L'équipe n° 1 britannique
désignée " l'équipe de l'année 1950 " par la presse britannique

CONTRE

U. S. COGNAÇAISE

A happy New Year to all our British Friends

DINER
DU 1ᵉʳ JANVIER 1952

OFFERT EN L'HONNEUR DE L'ÉQUIPE
PREMIÈRE DE RUGBY DU
NEWPORT ATHLETIC-CLUB
PAR LE
STADE NANTAIS UNIVERSITÉ CLUB
DANS LES SALONS DE L'HOTEL DE LA DUCHESSE-ANNE

Le Potage Crème Lison

Le Suprême de Bar Maréchal

Le Contrefilet Rôti à la Broche

Les Pommes Parisiennes

La Salade

La Glace Bombe Plombières

Les Gaufrettes

Les Vins Blanc et Médoc en Carafe
Le Muscadet 1948

Le Café

Hospitality in Cognac included a guided tour of a distillery. In the early eighteenth century an Irishman named Hennessy, together with a Mr Hine from Dorset and Mr Martell from the Channel Islands, arrived in the area and established cognac producing houses which were to become world famous. The Newport party visited the Hennessy distillery and were entertained by Mr Hennessy, a direct descendant of the firm's founder. The banquet held at the Brasserie Coq d'Or gave Bryn Williams a chance to distinguish himself by making a speech of thanks on behalf of the club in fluent French. The hospitality continued in Nantes as this dinner menu confirms.

A poster advertising the match at Nantes as a rugby international.

In September 1952, Newport played host to a combined Nantes/Cognac team, winning a closely fought game 12-11. In this photograph Gordon Keeley prepares to pass to Ken Jones.

MITCHELLS & BUTLERS

SOUTH AFRICA			NEWPORT		
Colours—Green and Gold			Colours—Black and Amber.		
J. BUCHLER	(1)	Full Back	Full Back	R. HUGHES	(1)
P. JOHNSTONE	(6)	Left Wing	Right Wing	KEN JONES	(2)
S. S. VIVIERS	(10)	Left Centre	Right Centre	MALCOLM THOMAS	(3)
R. van SCHOOR	(7)	Right Centre	Left Centre	BRYN WILLIAMS	(4)
F. MARAIS	(4)	Right Wing	Left Wing	JOHN LANE	(5)
D. J. FRY	(12)	Outside Half	Outside Half	ROY BURNETT, Capt.	(6)
P. A. du TOIT	(15)	Inside Half	Inside Half	W. A. WILLIAMS	(7)

Referee:
Mr. W. J. Evans,
Cardiff

NEXT HOME GAME—
v. COVENTRY
SATURDAY, JAN. 19th, 1952.
Kick-off 2.45 p.m.

Forwards—		Forwards—	
H. BEKKER	(21)	T. STERRY	(8)
W. DELPORT	(17)	LYN DAVIES	(9)
F. E. van der RYST	(19)	G. HIRST	(10)
B. MYBURGH	(28)	L. E. T. JONES	(11)
W. H. M. BARNARD	(25)	BEN EDWARDS	(12)
J. du RAND	(29)	PETER DAVIES	(14)
C. J. van WYK	(26)	D. G. ACKERMAN	(15)
H. MULLER, Capt.	(30)	H. J. TOVEY	(16)
Touch Judge—J. K. OCHSE		Touch Judge—R. T. CARTER	

MITCHELLS & BUTLERS

The Fourth Springboks met Newport on 10 January 1952. The previous Saturday they had beaten England 8-3 at Twickenham, giving them a Grand Slam over the four home countries which included the famous 44-0 defeat of Scotland. The match against Newport was the twenty-third of the tour and only London Counties had beaten the tourists. One late change in the Newport side shown in this programme saw Bobby Owen replace Bryn Williams in the centre. Williams had failed to recover from an injury sustained on the tour to France. It was not Newport's day, however, as an all-time record crowd at Rodney Parade of 31,000 saw the Springboks win 12-6, scoring four tries to Newport's one by Harry Tovey. Delighted with the victory, the 'Boks claimed to have played their best rugby of the tour. At the dinner held at the King's Head Hotel, R.T. Evans, who was unable to play due to injury, congratulated the visitors: 'We acknowledge that you are a great side and today you gave us a real object lesson in backing up. Hennie Muller gave us a perfect example of a number eight.'

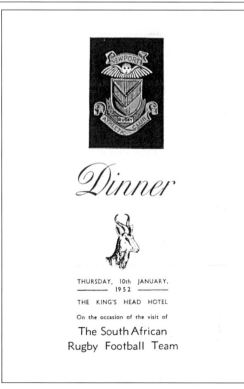

Dinner

THURSDAY, 10th JANUARY, 1952

THE KING'S HEAD HOTEL

On the occasion of the visit of

The South African
Rugby Football Team

South Africa versus Newport at Newport, 10 January 1952. From left to right (players only), back row : H. Bekker, W. Delport, W.H. Barnard, J. Du Rand, B. Myburgh, C. Van Wyck. Middle row: F. Van der Ryst, P. Du Toit, H. Muller (captain), B.S. Viviers, J. Buchler. Front row: P. Johnstone, R. Van Schoor, F.P. Marias, D.J. Fry.

Hennie Muller played international rugby between 1949 and 1953. Of his 13 Test appearances, 9 were as captain. In the third match of the tour at Pontypool Park, against a combined Pontypool/Newbridge side, Basil Kenyan had received an eye injury which required surgery and some months hospitalisation. Muller assumed the tour captaincy and led the Springboks in the Test matches and in the game at Rodney Parade. He made his Test debut against New Zealand in South Africa's first-post war international. Outstanding in a 15-11 victory, Hennie Muller went on to become one of the truly great Springboks and his performance at Rodney Parade will not be forgotten by those privileged to see it.

Newport First XV in 1951/52. R.T. 'Bob' Evans was team captain but an injury received at Abertillery in November subsequently forced him to retire from the game and Roy Burnett took over as leader. From left to right, back row: R. Lewis (hon. trainer), G. Hirst, T. Sterry, B. Edwards, P. Davies, L.E.T. Jones, A.H. Rowland, R. Hughes, R.T. Carter (match hon. secretary). Middle row: B. Williams, M.C. Thomas, V.J. Law (chairman), R.T. Evans (captain), W.A. Everson (football hon. secretary), R. Burnett (vice-captain), K. Jones. Front row: D.A.G. Ackerman, J. Lane, W.A. Williams, L. Davies.

As part of the Coronation celebrations in June 1953 a soccer match between Newport RFC and Newport County FC took place at Rodney Parade. Literally a game of two halves, a rugby ball was used in the first half and a soccer ball in the second. Of all the events organised by the council this was one of the few financial successes. An overall loss of £16,000 was made, which was largely blamed on the arrival of television. Season 1953/1954 saw Ken Jones in his second term as captain and the arrival of Onllwyn Brace, John Herrera and Brian Jones. The Newport squad was, from left to right, back row: R. Lewis (hon. trainer), M. Thomas, H. Davies, G. Morris, J. Herrera, M. Quartley, P. Smith, R. Sheppard, D. Ackerman, R. Carter (match hon. secretary). Middle row: G. Ross, R. Rowland, E.J. Shiner (chairman), K.J. Jones (captain), W.A. Everson (football hon. secretary), L. Davies (vice-captain), R. Burnett. Front row: R. Owen, D.O. Brace, B.J. Jones, J. Lane.

The 1953 Fourth New Zealand All Blacks. From left to right, back row: C.J. Loader, A.E.G. Elsom, J.W. Kelly, W.A. McCaw, K.L. Skinner, R.C. Hemi, J.M. Tanner, I.J. Clarke. Third row: C.A. Woods, H.L. White, R.A. White, P.F. Jones, K.P. Bagley, R.J. O'Dea, O.D. Oliver, G.N. Dalzell, W.H. Clark. Second row: R.A. Jarden, J.T. Fitgerald, D.D. Wilson, R.C. Stuart (captain), Mr J.N. Millard (manager), Mr A.E. Marslin (assistant manager), L.S. Haig (vice-captain), R.W.H. Scott, B.P. Eastgate, V.D. Bevan. Front row: B.B.J. Fitzpatrick, R.G. Bowers, K. Davis, M.J. Dixon, W.S.S. Freebairn.

How the teams lined up at Rodney Parade.

When the Fourth All Blacks came to town in
January they had suffered defeats against Wales
13-8 and Cardiff 8-3, while only drawing with
Swansea 6-6. The tour party contained household
names such as the captain R.C. Stuart, full-back
Bob Scott and loose forward Peter Jones. The party
also included a certain Brian Fitzpatrick playing at
second five-eighth (inside centre). Fitzpatrick
represented New Zealand in 3 Tests while his son,
Sean, would break all records, making 92 Test
appearances between 1986 and 1997, with 51 as
captain. An all-ticket crowd of 27,000 saw Newport
lose a tight match 11-6. A late drop goal by
D. Wilson clinched the win for New Zealand. The
forwards proved more than a match for the tourists,
although All Black forward Peter Jones produced
his best game of the tour. D.O. Brace received
numerous accolades for his performance at
scrum-half but the critics felt the Newport backs
failed to vary the game and make use of the pace
Ken Jones offered on the wing. The traditional after
match dinner was held at the King's Head Hotel.

New Zealand win the ball at a line-out. The
Newport players are, from the left: Davis,
Meredith, Herrera, Morris, Jenkins, Ackerman.

DINNER

THURSDAY, 21st JANUARY, 1954
AT THE KING'S HEAD HOTEL
On the occasion of the visit of

The New Zealand
Rugby Football Team

Chairman: E. J. SHINER, Esq.
(Chairman,
Newport Football Committee)

Kenneth Jeffrey Jones OBE made his debut for Newport in 1946. In his twelve seasons with the club he made 292 appearances and scored 145 tries before playing his final game at Llanelli on 24 April 1958. He was club captain for two seasons: 1950/51 and 1953/54. Ken's first Welsh cap was won against England on 18 January 1947 and he went on to play 43 consecutive games for Wales until he missed the England game on 19 January 1957 almost ten years to the date after his debut. He returned for his 44th and final appearance against Scotland. He captained Wales on a single occasion, in a victory over the Scots at St Helens, Swansea, in 1954. This was in recognition of his record-equalling 35th appearance for Wales. Perhaps his finest moment in a Welsh jersey was scoring the match-winning try against the Fourth All Blacks. He was seen collecting a cross-kick from Clem Thomas by a TV audience watching the first Welsh home international to be screened live. Ken Jones was a member of the 1950 British Isles touring side to New Zealand where he appeared in 3 Test matches. Ken's sporting achievements weren't confined to the rugby field. A world class sprinter, he won a silver medal in the 1948 Olympic Games held in London as a member of the 4x100 yards sprint relay team. He was also the Great Britain team captain at the 1954 European Games and a Welsh representative at the Empire and Commonwealth Games in Vancouver in the same year. He was manager of the Welsh team when Cardiff hosted the Empire and Commonwealth Games in 1958 and was given the honour of carrying the baton into the stadium at the opening ceremony.

NEWPORT ATHLETIC

CLUB

President: F. H. Dauncey, Esq.
Chairman: R. S. Snelling, Esq., J.P.

MEETING OF
MEMBERS OF THE CLUB
IN THE GYMNASIUM
ON 1st DECEMBER, 1954, AT 8 p.m.,
TO PAY TRIBUTE TO

KEN JONES

TO MARK HIS OUTSTANDING ATHLETIC
AND RUGBY FOOTBALL ACHIEVEMENTS

Principal Guest:
THE RT. HON. LORD ABERDARE,
G.B.E., LL.D., K.St.J.
(President of the British Empire and
Commonwealth Games Council for Wales)

KEN JONES

In December 1954 Ken Jones' sporting achievements were honoured by Newport Athletic Club. This was perhaps a little premature as more caps would be won. Top left and bottom are the cover and centre pages of a commemorative souvenir produced to mark the occasion. Top right is a card produced in the early 1950s. This is not a cigarette card but a weighing scales card – No. 6 of a series of 24 produced by The British Automatic Company Ltd of London.

Rugby Football

Played for Wales in 35 successive matches (breaking a record held by W. J. Bancroft, Swansea, of 33 successive Caps and equalling the record of R. Owen, of Swansea, who was Capped 35 times for Wales, but not on successive occasions)

Captained Wales against Scotland (1954)

Toured Australia and New Zealand with the British team, and played in all four Test Matches (1950)

Captain of Newport 1st XV, 1950-51 and 1953-54

Athletics

Represented Great Britain in Olympic Games in London (1948)

Captained British Team at the European Games at Berne (1954)

Represented Wales in Empire and Commonwealth Games at Vancouver (1954)

Represented England and Wales v. Scotland and Ireland at Manchester (1948)

Won Southern Counties A.A.A. 100 Yards' Championship (1948)

Welsh Sprint Champion, 100 Yards and 220 Yards, seven years in succession

---

Won United Provinces (India) Championship 100 and 200 Metres and Long Jump (1945)

Represented United Provinces (India) at All India Olympics at Bangalore (1946)

Won Northern University Championships 100 and 220 Yards (1949)

Won Loughborough College Championships 100 and 220 Yards (1949)

Victor Ludorum, West Mon. School, Pontypool (1939)

Joint Holder of English and Welsh Native 100 Yards' Record of 9.8 seconds

NEWPORT ATHLETIC CLUB

IRISH TOUR

2nd OCTOBER to 7th OCTOBER, 1954

Touring has always played a big part in the game of Rugby Union and Newport RFC is certainly no exception to this great tradition, with incoming tourists as regular visitors. The Barbarians RFC included a match at Rodney Parade as part of the Easter tour to South Wales and Newport has played host to many teams from developing countries. By the 1950s the club had started to tour both within the UK and Ireland and also into mainland Europe. In the 1970s, tours to North America and the southern hemisphere would also be made. In April 1954 the club toured Devon, where they had been frequent visitors, and on this occasion played Plymouth Albion, Devonport Services and Exeter. In October, Ireland was the destination with games against Lansdowne in Dublin and Dolphin in Cork. A similar tour had been made in 1953 but the first contact Newport had with Irish club rugby was in 1879 when South of Ireland visited Newport. This set a precedent as Queens College (Cork), Dublin Wanderers and Cork Constitution were all played in the latter part of the nineteenth century. This Irish tour brochure shows a very full itinerary.

ITINERARY

Saturday, 2nd October, 1954
7.40 p.m. Depart Newport. (Special Coach.
8.22 p.m. Depart Pontypool Road
       (Sandwiches and Coffee on Train)
11.21 p.m. Arrive Crewe.

Sunday, 3rd October, 1954
12.14 a.m. Depart Crewe. (Reserved accommodation)
2.35 a.m. Arrive Holyhead
3.25 a.m. Depart Holyhead
     (Sleeping Berths reserved on Steamer)
6.40 a.m. Arrive Dun Laoghaire
     (Party remain on board until 8.15 a.m.)
8.30 a.m. Party conveyed to Headquarters, Grosvenor Hotel,
     Dublin, by members of Lansdowne R.F.C.
9.0 a.m. Breakfast at Headquarters.
12.0 noon Leave for Greystones
1.0 p.m. Lunch at Grand Hotel, Greystones
     Sight seeing tours Greystones in afternoon
6.30 p.m. Dinner at Headquarters.
10.30 p.m. Bed (We hope)

Monday, 4th October, 1954
9.0 a.m. Breakfast
10.30 a.m. Leave for Mansion House
11.0 a.m. Civic Reception by Lord Mayor of Dublin
1.0 p.m. Lunch
3.45 p.m. Cars to Landsdowne Road Ground
4.45 p.m. Kick-off v. Landsdowne R.F.C.

7.30 p.m. Dinner at the Salthill Hotel, Monkstown,
       Guests of Landsdowne R.F.C

Tuesday, 5th October, 1954
7.45 a.m. Breakfast
8.15 a.m. Depart Hotel for Kingsbridge Station
8.45 a.m. Depart Dublin for Cork. (Reserved accommodation)
12.0 noon Arrive Glanmire Road Station, Cork
     Party met by members of Dolphin R.F.C.
1.0 p.m. Lunch, Metropole Hotel (Headquarters)
7.0 p.m. Dolphin R.F.C. Dinner to party, Metropole Hotel

Wednesday, 6th October, 1954
9.0 a.m. Breakfast
1.0 p.m. Lunch
2.15 p.m. Coach to Musgrave Park
3.0 p.m. Kick-off v. Dolphin R.F.C.
4.15 p.m. Light refreshments
5.15 p.m. Coach from Musgrave Park to Hotel Metropole
5.30 p.m. Coach from Metropole Hotel to Fishguard Boat
6.0 p.m. Depart Cork for Fishguard
     (Dinner on board m.v. " Innisfallen Way ")

Thursday, 7th October, 1954
3.30 a.m. Arrive Fishguard
4.55 a.m. Leave Fishguard. (Breakfast on Train)
8.32 a.m. Arrive Newport

Our Chairman, Mr. W. H. Bryant (who apologizes for absence) and Committee wish you a successful and enjoyable trip.

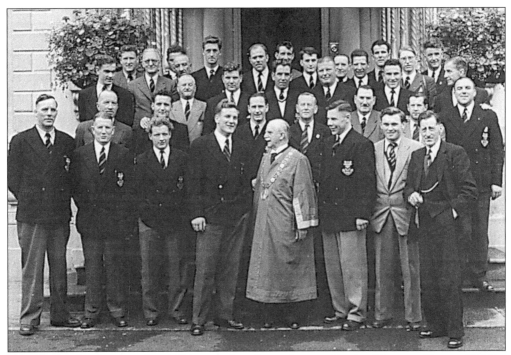

A photograph taken on the 1954 tour, thought to be outside the Mansion House, Dublin, showing a group of Newport players and officials with the Lord Mayor.

The team that defeated Dolphin 25-15. From left to right, back row: Irish match official, F. Cox, R. Sheppard, E. Pryor, G. Morris, I. Ford, J. Lane, J. Wills, P. Smith, M. Thomas, R.T. Evans. Middle row: M. Quartley, L. Davies, K.J. Jones, R. Rowland. Front row: D. Ackerman, J. Thomas, R. Burnett.

Menu

Hors d'Oeuvres

Cream of Celery Soup
or
Chicken Consomme

Grilled Fresh Tamar Salmon
Cucumber and Butter Sauce

Fillet of Beef Steak
Button Mushrooms and Tomato
French Fried Potatoes

Roast Devon Turkey
Bread Sauce—Savoury Stuffing
Sweet Garden Peas
Croquette Potatoes

Californian Fresh Fruit
Salad
with
Maraschino

Assorted Cheeses
and
Biscuits

Coffee

NEWPORT ATHLETIC CLUB

Dinner

at

THE DUKE OF CORNWALL HOTEL
PLYMOUTH

Kick-off 7 p.m.   Sunday 4th April, 1954

Menu card for an official dinner on the tour to Devon in 1954. The alternative fare offered makes interesting reading.

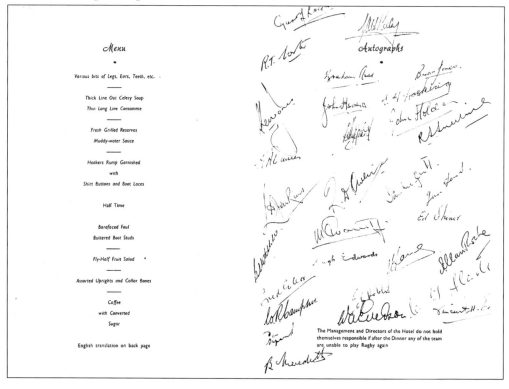

Menu

Various bits of Legs, Ears, Teeth, etc.

Thick Line Out Celery Soup
Thin Long Line Consomme

Fresh Grilled Reserves
Muddy-water Sauce

Hookers Rump Garnished
with
Shirt Buttons and Boot Laces

Half Time

Barefaced Foul
Buttered Boot Studs

Fly-Half Fruit Salad

Assorted Uprights and Collar Bones

Coffee
with Converted
Sugar

English translation on back page

Autographs

The Management and Directors of the Hotel do not hold
themselves responsible if after the Dinner any of the team
are unable to play Rugby again

The oldest Anglo-Welsh first-class club fixture is Newport versus Blackheath, which was first played in 1879 when the English side became the first team to beat Newport. February 1953 saw the occasion of the 100th match in this series of fixtures. The game was played at Rodney Parade and guests at a celebratory dinner included Brigadier H.L. Glyn Hughes CBE, DSO, president of Blackheath, Councillor L.F.A. Driscoll, deputy mayor of Newport, and Danny Davies of the WRU. Of the 100 games played, Newport had won 78, Blackheath 15 and 7 were drawn.

DINNER

SATURDAY, 28th FEBRUARY, 1953

in

THE GYMNASIUM, RODNEY ROAD,

NEWPORT

6 p.m.

On the Occasion of the

One Hundredth Match

between

Newport and Blackheath

Chairman:

A. R. TOVEY, Esq.

(Chairman, Newport Football Committee)

When Ken Jones made his record-breaking 43rd consecutive appearance for Wales, seven of his Newport team-mates were there to help him celebrate. Jones' 43 caps was a British record at the time, the previous holder being George Stephenson of Ireland. In this photograph, Ken Jones is joined by, from left to right, back row: G. Owen, B.V. Meredith, L.H. Jenkins, M.C. Thomas. Front row: G. Whitson, K.J. Jones, D.O. Brace, H.P. Morgan. For the record, Wales defeated France 5-3 with Garfield Owen converting a late Welsh try to win the game.

The First XV photograph for 1957/58 includes all members of the team which defeated the Australian tourists. Only H.P. Morgan, J. Roblin and J. Herrera were absent. From left to right, back row: R. Lewis (attendant), M.C. Thomas, B. Cresswell, J. Herrera, I. Ford, G. Davidge, G. Whitson, N. Morgan, R.T. Carter (match secretary). Seated: B.V. Meredith, K.J. Jones, V.J. Parfitt (chairman), L.H. Jenkins (captain), W.A. Everson (football hon. secretary), D. Greenslade, J. Phillips. Front row: H.P. Morgan, B.J. Jones, J. Roblin, J. Hurrell, R. Burnett, B. Scrivens.

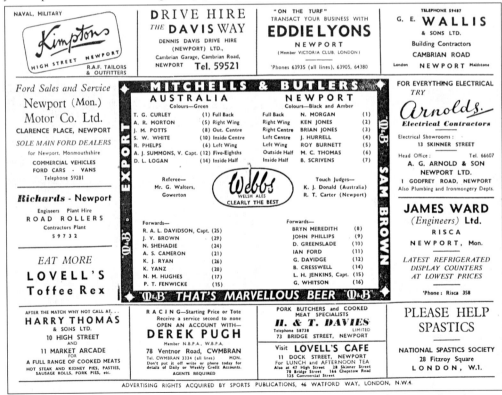

The Australia and Newport teams. G.D. Bailey replaced J.M. Potts in the Australian line-up. Newport won the game 11-0 with tries by Hurrell and Jenkins with Morgan adding a conversion and dropped goal.

The Australian team that were beaten at Rodney Parade. From left to right, back row: N. Hughes, N. Shehadie, A. Cameron, K. Ryan, T. Curley, G. Bailey. Middle row: J. Brown, A. Summons, R. Davidson (captain), K. Yanz, P. Fenwicke. Front row: R. Phelps, A. Morton, D. Logan, S. White.

In a Test career spanning eleven years, Nicholas Shehadie was a member of both the third and fourth Australian touring sides to the UK. At the end of the 1947/48 tour he played against the Barbarians on the first occasion that the famous club played against international tourists. Ten years later he was honoured by the Barbarians when selected to play against Australia in the end-of-tour match. He was the first overseas player to receive this accolade. After retiring from the game his involvement in rugby continued. He managed Australia on overseas tours and became president of the Australian RFU in 1980.

Newport supplied the Welsh back row for the match against Scotland at Cardiff on 6 February 1960. All three players had previously been capped, but this was the first of two matches in which they would appear as a unit. From left to right: Geoff Whitson played 3 times for Wales; Glyn Davidge won 9 caps; Brian Cresswell appeared 4 times and scored 2 tries.

Two
1963 and All That

The Newport squad that won the 1961 Welsh seven-a-side tournament at Cardiff on 29 April. From left to right, back row: G. Lewis (hon. trainer), R. Wills, G. Whitson, B. Price, G. Davidge, B.V. Meredith, R.T. Carter (match hon. secretary). Middle row: G. Britton, R.T. Evans (chairman), B.J. Jones (captain), W.A. Everson (hon. secretary), G. Davies. Front row: J. Ryan, G. Bevan.

Seven-a-side rugby was first played in Scotland in 1883. Tournaments had proved popular at Melrose, Gala and Hawick among others and in 1926 the Middlesex Sevens was introduced at Twickenham. Newport had been a guest side at Twickenham in 1949, losing in the semi-final, and it was fitting that a Welsh tournament should begin at Rodney Parade. In 1954 Newport hosted the first Welsh seven-a-side tournament. Under the guidance of Bill Everson, a committee representing the leading sixteen Welsh clubs had proposed the new event to the WRU. R.S. Snelling, then president of Newport Athletic Club, donated a trophy and the event was held at the end of the season. The tournament ran for forty-two years and was last held in Cardiff in 1995. A congested fixture list was blamed for its eventual demise and the trophy was returned to Newport for posterity. Newport won the first event by beating Ebbw Vale in the final 6-0. The club became the most successful in the history of the tournament, winners on 10 occasions and runners-up 9 times. The early years of the tournament saw Newport at its best, appearing in 12 of the first 15 finals and winning 9. The club produced some great exponents of the game – Ken Jones, Roy Burnett and Malcolm Thomas excelled in the 1950s and were followed by Brian Jones, David Watkins and Byron Thomas in the 1960s. Not just a game for pacy and mercurial backs, forwards Brian Price, Bryn Meredith and Glyn Davidge among others revelled in the open spaces and delighted the crowds with their ball-in-hand skills. Newport achieved a hat-trick of wins in 1961, 1962 and 1963, but were not able to maintain their early successes. After beating Cardiff 21-15 in the 1967 final, Newport had to wait until 1985 for the tenth and last success, beating Glamorgan Wanderers 43-0. This photograph shows the first winners of the tournament in 1954. From left to right, back row: L. Davies, M.C. Thomas, R. Sheppard, M. Quartley, D.A.G. Ackerman, B. Williams. Front row: G. Ross, K.J. Jones, Mr E. Shiner (chairman), B.J. Jones, R. Burnett.

At St Helens, Swansea, in April 1962, Newport recorded their sixth success in the tournament. A crowd of 20,000 saw Newport beat Neath 19-3 in the final. This photograph of the winners shows, from left to right, back row: Byron Thomas, Glyn Davidge, Bryn Meredith (captain, holding trophy), Brian Price, Brian Jones. Front row: Bob Prosser and David Watkins.

This programme shows Newport's path to winning the 1962 trophy.

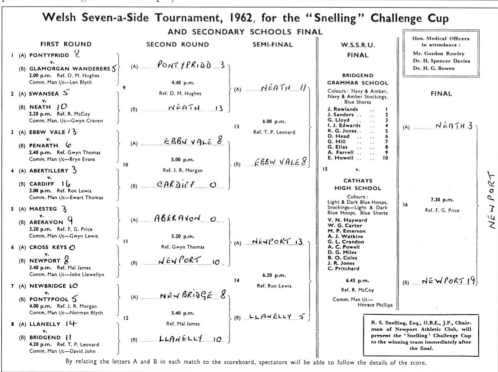

Welsh Seven-a-Side Tournament, 1962, for the "Snelling" Challenge Cup
AND SECONDARY SCHOOLS FINAL

FIRST ROUND	SECOND ROUND	SEMI-FINAL	W.S.S.R.U. FINAL	FINAL
1 (A) PONTYPRIDD 2				Hon. Medical Officers in attendance:
v.	(A) PONTYPRIDD 3			Mr. Gordon Rowley
(B) GLAMORGAN WANDERERS 5				Dr. H. Spencer Davies
2.00 p.m. Ref. D. M. Hughes Comm. Man i/c—Len Blyth	4.40 p.m.	(A) NEATH 11	BRIDGEND GRAMMAR SCHOOL	Dr. H. G. Bowen
2 (A) SWANSEA 5	Ref. D. M. Hughes		Colours: Navy & Amber, Navy & Amber Stockings, Blue Shorts	FINAL
v.	(B) NEATH 13		J. Rowlands .. 1	
(B) NEATH 10			J. Sanders .. 2	
2.20 p.m. Ref. R. McCoy Comm. Man i/c—Gwyn Craven			G. Lloyd .. 3	
3 (A) EBBW VALE 13	(A) EBBW VALE 8	6.00 p.m.	I. J. Edwards .. 4	(A) NEATH 3
v.		Ref. T. P. Leonard	K. G. Jones .. 5	
(B) PENARTH 6			D. Head .. 6	
2.40 p.m. Ref. Gwyn Thomas Comm. Man i/c—Bryn Evans	5.00 p.m.	(B) EBBW VALE 8	G. Hill .. 7	
4 (A) ABERTILLERY 3	Ref. J. R. Morgan		G. Elias .. 8	
v.			A. Farrell .. 9	
(B) CARDIFF 16	(B) CARDIFF 0		E. Howell .. 10	
3.00 p.m. Ref. Ron Lewis Comm. Man i/c—Ewart Thomas			v.	
5 (A) MAESTEG 3			CATHAYS HIGH SCHOOL	7.30 p.m.
v.	(A) ABERAVON 0		Colours: Light & Dark Blue Hoops, Stockings—Light & Dark Blue Hoops, Blue Shorts	Ref. F. G. Price
(B) ABERAVON 9			V. N. Hayward	
3.20 p.m. Ref. F. G. Price Comm. Man i/c—Gwyn Lewis	5.20 p.m.	(A) NEWPORT 13	W. G. Carter	
6 (A) CROSS KEYS 0	Ref. Gwyn Thomas		M. P. Emerson	
v.			A. J. Watkins	
(B) NEWPORT 8	(B) NEWPORT 10		G. L. Crandon	
3.40 p.m. Ref. Mal James Comm. Man i/c—John Llewellyn			A. C. Powell	
7 (A) NEWBRIDGE 10		6.20 p.m.	D. G. Miles	
v.	(A) NEWBRIDGE 8	Ref. Ron Lewis	B. O. Coles	(B) NEWPORT 19
(B) PONTYPOOL 5			J. R. Jones	
4.00 p.m. Ref. J. R. Morgan Comm. Man i/c—Norman Blyth	5.40 p.m.	(B) LLANELLY 5	C. Pritchard	
8 (A) LLANELLY 14	Ref. Mal James		6.45 p.m. Ref. R. McCoy	
v.			Comm. Man i/c— Horace Phillips	
(B) BRIDGEND 11	(B) LLANELLY 10			
4.20 p.m. Ref. T. P. Leonard Comm. Man i/c—David John				

R. S. Snelling, Esq., O.B.E., J.P., Chairman of Newport Athletic Club, will present the 'Snelling' Challenge Cup to the winning team immediately after the final.

By relating the letters A and B in each match to the scoreboard, spectators will be able to follow the details of the score.

The hat-trick of wins achieved by Newport in 1963 was marred by the death of Mr R.S. Snelling OBE, president of the seven-a-side committee, four days earlier. This time Glyn Davidge was captain and the only change from 1962 saw Graham Bevan replace Bryn Meredith. Davidge is up on the shoulders of Brian Price and Brian Jones.

By 1965 there were some changes in personnel. David Watkins was now captain and Alan Thomas, Brian Perrins, Stuart Watkins and Gordon Britton, who had played in the 1961 winning side, were in the team. In the first 12 tournaments Newport had won 40 games and lost 4. From left to right, back row: A. Thomas, B. Price, S. Watkins, G. Britton, G. Lewis (trainer). Front row: B. Perrins, D. Watkins, R. Prosser.

A product of West Mon Grammar School, Bryn Meredith made his Newport debut in 1951/52. Over the next ten years he would gain a worldwide reputation as an outstanding forward. His three overseas tours with the British Isles, to South Africa in 1955 and 1962 and Australia and New Zealand in 1959, introduced the southern hemisphere to his skills. Although he appeared in the 8 Test matches on his two visits to South Africa, he was denied a Test match in 1959. Tour captain Ronnie Dawson of Ireland claimed the position, although Meredith's superiority as a hooker and player in general has always been recognised. He led Newport during 1958/59 and 1961/62 and was Welsh captain on 4 occasions. His 34 caps was a record number for a hooker, only recently broken by Garin Jenkins of Swansea.

Glyn Davidge went to South Africa as a replacement on the 1962 British Isles tour, represented Wales 9 times and was club captain in 1962/63. Despite all the above honours, it will be for two games that Glyn will be best remembered. Against South Africa in 1961 and New Zealand in 1963 he put in performances which have entered into the folklore of Newport RFC. To say he 'died' for the club is stretching it a bit – particularly as he is regularly seen in the clubhouse on match days. However, he did all and more for the black and ambers on these two occasions. 'In the mauls there was Davidge, a heroic figure, as his bruised body testified' wrote J.B.G. Thomas in his report on the victory over the All Blacks. Davidge played 270 games in the famous colours and, whether at number eight or on the flank, he always led from the front.

The South African tourists, 1960/61. From left to right, back row: F. du Preez, Hugo Van Zyl, A. Baard, Piet Van Zyl, Hennie Van Zyl, H. Van Der Merwe, D. Stewart, M. Pelser, M. Antelme. Third row: R. Hill, Abe Malan, J. Gainsford, J. Engelbreght, H. Botha, J. Myburgh, D. Hopwood, L. Wilson, D. Holton, F. Kuhn. Second row: J. Claassen, I. Kirkpatrick, Avril Malan (captain), Mr 'Ferdie' Bergh (manager), R. Lockyear (vice-captain), Mr 'Boy' Louw (assistant manager), P. du Toit. Front row: C. Nimb, P. Uys, F. Roux, B. Van Niekerk, K. Oxlee, G. Wentzel. Newport met the Fifth Springboks on 11 January 1961. It was the twenty-fourth match of the tour. Only the Midland Counties had held the tourists, gaining a 3-3 draw at Leicester in the fifth match on 5 November. The team provided tremendous opposition and could, and probably should, have won. An early try for the visitors by lock forward Piet Van Zyl was the only score of the game. Newport had four penalty kicks at goal without success and a drop goal attempt by Billy Watkins fell beneath the cross bar. It was particularly unfortunate that Norman Morgan, the regular goal kicker and then current record point scorer for the club, had to miss the match through injury. While nothing is guaranteed when it comes to place kicks, all the missed efforts fell comfortably within Morgan's ability. J.B.G. Thomas wrote: 'I have never seen the Newport pack play better in thirty years and every one of the eight gave of their very best in a truly magnificent display. Glyn Davidge as the pack leader was outstanding and gave a performance not likely to be equalled by any of his club mates for many years to come.' The Springboks tour continued its winning run until the thirtieth and final match of the British sector of the tour. The Barbarians became the only side to defeat the tourists by winning 6-0 at Cardiff Arms Park on 4 February. Brian Jones, Brian Price and Billy Watkins were Newport's representatives in the Barbarians team.

SOUTH AFRICA					NEWPORT	
Colours : Green and Gold					Colours : Black and Amber	
L. G. WILSON	29	Full Back		Full Back	B. EDWARDS	1
H. J. van ZYL	25	Left Wing		Right Wing	C. LEWIS	2
B. B. van NIEKERK	23	Left Centre		Right Centre	G. BRITTON	3
A. I. KIRKPATRICK	21	Right Centre		Left Centre	B. J. JONES (Capt.)	4
M. J. G. ANTELME	26	Right Wing		Left Wing	P. REES	5
K. OXLEE	19	Outside Half		Outside Half	W. GRIFFITHS	6
P. de W. UYS	18	Inside Half		Inside Half	W. R. WATKINS	7
S. P. KUHN	1	Forwards		Forwards	D. GREENSLADE	8
R. JOHNS	6				B. MEREDITH	9
J. L. MYBURGH	2				N. JOHNSON	10
P. J. van ZYL	10		Referee : Mr. G. THOMAS, Aberporth		I. FORD	11
J. T. CLAASSEN	8				B. PRICE	12
H. S. van der MERWE	9		Touch Judges :		B. CRESSWELL	14
A. S. MALAN (Capt.)	7		Mr. D. A. STEWART		G. DAVIDGE	15
D. J. HOPWOOD	15		Mr. R. T. CARTER		G. WHITSON	16

NEXT HOME GAME v. *Swansea* SATURDAY 14th JANUARY, 1960, Kick-off 3.15 p.m.

This programme shows the team line-ups for the match. One late change in the South African side saw G.H. Van Zyl replace H.S. Van der Merwe in the back row. Throughout their history, Newport RFC had always numbered the side starting with number one at full-back. Tradition had also dictated that number thirteen would not be used, resulting in a back row numbered fourteen, fifteen and sixteen. The International Board agreed that all international teams would be numbered one to fifteen, starting from the loose-head prop through to full-back. This commenced in 1960/61. Newport decided to adopt this system and the match against Penarth on 1 September 1962 saw it introduced. Centre Gordon Britton became the first player in the club's history to pull on a black and amber jersey with number thirteen on the back.

Season 1961/62 saw the arrival at the club of four players who would make a huge impact in the following years. A new half-back partnership established itself, with David Watkins and Bob Prosser becoming great favourites of the supporters, and John Uzzell slotted well into the centre as Brian Jones' partner. Alan Thomas joined Cresswell and Davidge in the back row. This is the 1961/62 Newport squad. From left to right, back row: G. Lewis (attendant), J. Anderson, N. Johnson, D. Greenslade, I. Ford, B. Price, B. Cresswell, N. Morgan, A. Thomas, R.T. Carter (match secretary). Middle row: P. Rees, D. Perrott, B.V. Williams (chairman), B. Meredith (captain), W.A. Everson (football hon. secretary), G. Davidge, B.J. Jones. Front row: J. Uzzell, D. Watkins, R. Prosser, B. Edwards.

The Fifth New Zealand All Blacks arrived in Newport for the third match of their tour to the British Isles, France and Canada. Oxford University (19-3) and Southern Counties (32-3) had been comfortably beaten and the tourists started favourites to beat a Newport side who had begun the 1963/64 season in mediocre form. Of the 12 matches played to date, only 6 had been won with 4 losses against Bristol, Neath, Cardiff and Gloucester. Before a packed house at Rodney Parade on a miserable and wet Wednesday afternoon, Newport gained their first win over New Zealand to rank alongside victories over South Africa (1912) and Australia (1957) and complete a unique treble. The New Zealand side led by Wilson Whineray included the world's most prolific goal kicker, Don Clarke, together with his brother Ian and one of the best back row units the game has seen: Waka Nathan, Brian Lochore and Kel Tremain. The result of the game – Newport winning 3-0 thanks to a John Uzzell drop goal – is well documented but it was only four months later, after the All Blacks had completed a 36-match itinerary, that the importance of the result could be put in perspective. The full tour record shows that of 36 matches played, 34 were won with a 0-0 draw against Scotland and the defeat at Newport. The All Blacks scored 613 points and conceded 159. This photograph of the Fifth All Blacks contains, from left to right, back row: C.R. Laidlaw, W.L. Davis, D.J. Graham, R.W. Caulton, P.F. Little, J.M. Le Lievre, W.J. Nathan, I.S.T. Smith, P.T. Walsh. Third row: I.R. Macrae, K.E. Barry, K.A. Nelson, S.T. Meads, C.E. Meads, A.J. Stewart, R.H. Horsley, B.J. Lochore, K.F. Gray, K.R. Tremain. Second row: D.A. Arnold, I.J. Clarke, D.B. Clarke, K.C. Briscoe, F.D. Kilby (manager), W.J. Whineray (captain), N.J. McPhail (assistant manager), D. Young, E.W. Kirton, J. Major, M.J. Dick. Front row: B.A. Watt, M.A. Herewini.

No book on Newport RFC would be complete without this photograph. It has been reproduced on numerous occasions and was chosen for the cover of *One Hundred Years of Newport Rugby*. All eyes are raised skywards as John Uzzell's drop goal clears the crossbar. Easily identified are, from left to right: Neville Johnson (arms raised), Ian Ford and David Jones, Kel Tremain, Ron Horsley, Waka Nathan, referee Gwyn Walters, Ian Clarke, Keith Poole and, to the right of the uprights, New Zealand captain Wilson Whineray.

NEW ZEALAND				NEWPORT	
Colours : All Black				Colours : Black and Amber	
D. B. CLARKE	(1)	Full Back	Full Back	R. CHENEY	(15)
R. W. CAULTON	(2)	Left Wing	Right Wing	S. WATKINS	(14)
P. T. WALSH	(8)	Left Centre	Right Centre	J. UZZELL	(13)
I. R. MACRAE	(7)	Right Centre	Left Centre	B. J. JONES	(12)
W. L. DAVIS	(6)	Right Wing	Left Wing	D. PERROTT	(11)
E. W. KIRTON	(10)	Outside Half	Outside Half	D. WATKINS	(10)
K. C. BRISCOE	(11)	Inside Half	Inside Half	W. R. PROSSER	(9)
W. J. WHINERAY (Capt.)	(17)	Forwards	Forwards	N. JOHNSON	(1)
J. MAJOR	(16)			G. BEVAN	(2)
I. J. CLARKE	(18)			D. JONES	(3)
R. H. HORSLEY	(20)			B. V. PRICE (Capt.)	(4)
C. E. MEADS	(22)			I. FORD	(5)
W. J. NATHAN	(25)			A. THOMAS	(6)
B. J. LOCHORE	(28)			G. DAVIDGE	(8)
K. R. TREMAIN	(30)			K. W. POOLE	(7)

Touch Judge : Mr. D. J. GRAHAM   Referee : Mr. G. WALTERS - Gowerton   Touch Judge : Mr. R. T. CARTER

NEXT HOME GAME : v. **Ebbw Vale**   SATURDAY, 2nd NOVEMBER, 1963, Kick-off 3.15 p.m.

How the teams lined up.

The Newport team that defeated New Zealand. From left to right, back row: D. Jones, K. Poole, G. Davidge, I. Ford, S.J. Watkins, N. Johnson, R.T. Carter (touch judge). Middle row: D. Perrott, G. Bevan, B. Price (captain), B.J. Jones, R. Cheyney. Front row: A. Thomas, D. Watkins, W.R. Prosser, J. Uzzell.

The press applauded Newport's victory and the original of this cartoon was presented to the club.

Driven to the ground by Ian Ford and Graham Bevan, Kel Tremain loses the ball and Colin 'Pinetree' Meads moves in to pick up the scraps. To be chosen as your country's Player of the Century is a special achievement and when that country is New Zealand it's even more special. This accolade, voted for by the nation's rugby public, was given to Colin Meads as the twentieth century came to an end. In 55 Test matches between 1958 and 1971 Meads strutted his stuff around the rugby globe and left his mark in every major rugby-playing country. Although a loser at Newport, he was quick to give the winning side the credit they deserved. His only other contact with Newport came at Auckland in 1966 when David Watkins was the captain of the British Isles in the fourth Test. Unseen by the referee, he was floored by Meads, who later claimed that Watkins had struck first! He became only the second player to be sent off in an international, against Scotland at Murrayfield in 1967, so a whiter-than-white All Black he certainly wasn't. However, the legend lives on and Colin Meads' place in rugby history is assured.

The lost art of line-out jumping is perfectly demonstrated by Newport's captain Brian Price. A great exponent of the line-out, Price wins the ball from Horsley while in the background Nathan, Poole and Thomas watch on. Brian Price made his international debut against Ireland in 1961 and went on to win 32 caps. He captained Wales in 6 internationals and led the first Welsh side to tour New Zealand and Australia in 1969. He also toured down under with the British Isles in 1966, appearing in 4 Tests.

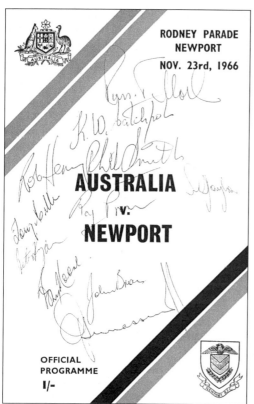

RODNEY PARADE
NEWPORT
NOV. 23rd, 1966

AUSTRALIA
v.
NEWPORT

OFFICIAL
PROGRAMME
1/-

The Australian tourists that visited Newport in November 1966 suffered extremely mixed fortunes during their 30-match tour. Captain John Thornett missed several games due to a contagious skin infection and hooker Ross Cullen was sent home by the management for an ear-biting incident in the third match against Oxford University. Only 15 matches were won with 13 defeats and 2 draws. A first-ever victory over Wales and wins against England and the Barbarians proved to be the tour highlights. The 3-3 draw at Rodney Parade was a great disappointment as injury saw Newport reduced to thirteen players. Centres Gordon Britton and David Cornwall both left the field with Britton's injury causing great concern to all present. He was resuscitated on the field after a collision of heads and happily made a full recovery. The selection of the Welsh XV to play the tourists ten days later was very controversial. It saw Newport's David Watkins replaced in the side by Barry John, then of Llanelli, who won his first cap.

The Newport team that played Australia, from left to right, back row: A. Panting (match secretary), A. Thomas, J. Anthony, B. Price, W. Morris, H. Jones, K. Poole, P.J. Hill (chairman). Middle row: M. Webber, S. Watkins, D. Watkins (captain), B. Perrins, G. Britton. Front row: D. Cornwall, D. Perrott, P. Watts, V. Perrins.

Stuart Watkins was a member of the Newport side that defeated the 1963 All Blacks. It was from his cross-kick that the ball was set up for John Uzzell to drop the winning goal. He joined Newport from Cross Keys at the start of the 1963/64 season and in his six seasons with the club, Watkins made 162 appearances and scored 115 tries. He played on the right wing for Wales in 26 matches and toured Australia and New Zealand with the British Isles in 1966, appearing in 3 Test matches.

Keith Jarrett was an eighteen-year-old schoolboy when he made his debut for Newport at Ebbw Vale on 24 December 1966. A product of Monmouth School, he had made a name for himself as a prolific goal kicker and had attracted the attention of several leading clubs. He started the 1966/67 season at Abertillery but soon moved down the valley to Rodney Parade. In September 1969 Jarrett's Rugby Union career ended when he signed to play Rugby League for northern club Barrow for a fee of £14,000. In his 82 appearances for Newport he scored 584 points, made up of 28 tries, 86 penalty goals and 121 conversions. He won 10 Welsh caps, toured Australia and New Zealand with Wales in 1969 and was a member of the 1968 British Isles team in South Africa. In this photograph Jarrett fields the ball in a Bank Holiday fixture with London Welsh on 7 April 1969. The London Welsh players are Geoff Evans, Mervyn Davies and John Taylor.

Keith Jarrett's Welsh debut comes straight off the pages of a *Boys Own* story. One month short of his nineteenth birthday he was selected to play out of position at full-back in the last game of the 1966/67 season. On 15 April, Wales played England at Cardiff Arms Park needing to win to avoid a whitewash while England needed victory for a Triple Crown. Keith Jarrett scored a record equalling 19 points, including a spectacular individual try. After fielding the ball in the Welsh half of the field, Jarrett ran up the left touchline outpacing the opposition to score in the corner. The conversion opened up a 9-point lead for Wales which effectively saw off the English challenge. This picture shows what appears to be a tie-wearers' convention with the scoreboard illustrating the final score.

Among many telegrams received, both wishing good luck before the match and congratulations after, Keith Jarrett received this from an English supporter.

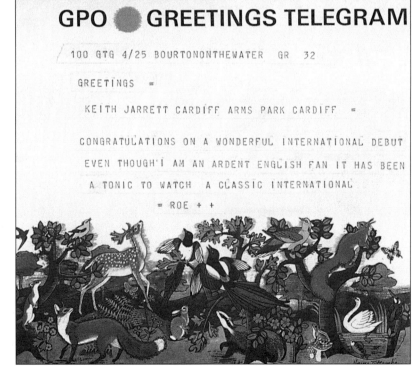

GPO ● GREETINGS TELEGRAM

100 GTG 4/25 BOURTONONTHEWATER   GR   32

GREETINGS =

KEITH JARRETT CARDIFF ARMS PARK CARDIFF   =

CONGRATULATIONS ON A WONDERFUL INTERNATIONAL DEBUT

EVEN THOUGH I AM AN ARDENT ENGLISH FAN IT HAS BEEN

A TONIC TO WATCH A CLASSIC INTERNATIONAL

= ROE + +

Congratulations poured in after Jarrett's debut. This letter was received from Newport Member of Parliament Roy Hughes. After he made the decision to play Rugby League, Clem Thomas wrote in *The Guardian*: 'To my mind the loss of Jarrett is grievous, for I believe that on the recent tour of the Antipodes he had finished his apprenticeship and emerged as a centre of the highest class. So much so that I believe him now to be the best centre in the world.' In 1973 Keith Jarrett's rugby career was brought to a premature end when he suffered the first of three strokes. Happily recovered, he can look back with great pride to his playing days and that incredible debut.

House of Commons,
London, S.W.1

17ᵗʰ April, 1967

Dear Keith,
Just a note to let you know that I was delighted to watch your performance for Wales last Saturday. You certainly brought great credit to Newport. Best wishes for your future career,
Yours sincerely,
Roy Hughes
Member for Newport.

"If you don't want to lose all Wales in the next election you'd better give Keith Jarrett a knighthood."

Arriving at the bus station after the match Keith found he had missed the last bus. Realising who he was, an inspector told a driver to get a bus and take him home to Newport. Moments later a single-decker pulled up. The inspector remonstrated with the driver, 'Take it back Dai and bring a double-decker. Mr Jarrett may want to smoke!'

The Newport-Cardiff fixture has been in existence for approximately 125 years. The records retained by the clubs are not in total agreement on the number of matches played or, indeed, when 'battle' commenced. Newport records show three matches played against Cardiff in 1875/76 but statistics produced by Cardiff club historian Danny Davies in his centenary book begin in 1876/77. A further anomaly concerns the Electric Light Match played at Newport on 16 December 1878. This match is not recognised in the Cardiff records. While not claiming to be completely accurate to the satisfaction of both clubs, it is suggested that at the end of the 1999/2000 season Newport and Cardiff had met on 383 occasions, Cardiff had won 185 games, Newport 139 and 59 had been drawn. For many years the clubs played each other four times. To maintain the consistency over a season and gain four victories proved very difficult. Cardiff achieved this on four occasions – 1897/98, 1905/06, 1947/48 and 1951/52 – while Newport, sadly, have never managed this feat, coming close 9 times with 3 wins and a draw. In the modern game it seems unlikely that the clubs will play 4 matches in a season again. The last time Newport went into the fourth match with three wins in the bag was on 16 April 1969. This fixture had been postponed earlier in the season due to bad weather but conditions were perfect for rugby on a Wednesday night that saw the crowds pour into Cardiff Arms Park. Four days earlier Wales had defeated England 30-9 with Maurice Richards scoring 4 tries. Brian Price was forced to step down from the Welsh side due to an injury which also prevented him appearing against Cardiff. The Arms Park was being redeveloped and all spectators were on the south side of the ground, looking beyond the field of play at a building site. Although they outscored Cardiff by two tries to one, Newport could only gain a 9-9 draw. Gareth Edwards scored all Cardiff's points with a try and two penalty goals while Barry Llewellyn and Stuart Watkins scored tries for Newport with Keith Jarrett adding a penalty. To rub salt in the wound, one of Jarrett's conversion attempts hit an upright. The Newport team shown here is, from left to right, back row: B. Llewellyn, K. Jarrett, K. Poole, T. Davies, J. Jeffery, J. Watkins, W. Morris, B. Price (club captain), Mr G. Walters (referee). Middle row: I. Taylor, V. Perrins, D. Haines, S. Watkins (captain), P. Rees, R. Phillips, J. Anthony. Front row: G. Treharne.

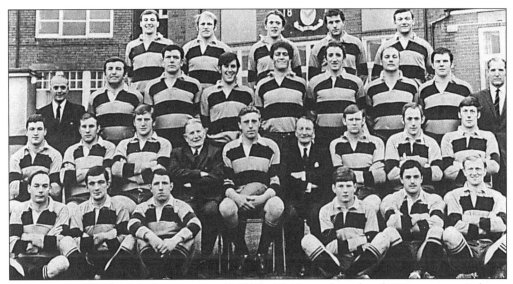

Newport were Welsh club champions in 1968/69. Of 45 matches played, 38 were won, 3 drawn and 4 lost. A record-equalling 716 points were scored with 309 points conceded. The Newport squad are, from left to right, back row: K. Poole, D. Cornwall, R. Phillips, A. Skirving, V. Perrins. Third row: R. Davies (trainer), C. Prescott, L. Martin, T. Davies, W. Morris, J. Watkins, G. Jones, G. Sutton, A.J. Panting (match hon. secretary). Second row: K. Jarrett, P. Watts, B. Llewellyn, R.T. Carter (football hon. secretary), B. Price (captain), H. Saysell (chairman), S. Watkins, D. Haines, J. Jeffery. Front row: D. Perrott, B. Mills, I. Taylor, M. Parry, P. Evans, G. Treharne.

Season 1968/69 saw club records tumble. Keith Jarrett rewrote the individual record books, becoming the highest points scorer in a season with 250, scorer of the most points in a match with 30 against Penarth and the scorer of the fastest century of points – taking only 9 games to score 102. The team's 38 victories were the most recorded in a season, beating the 37 achieved in 1950/51, and the final table shown makes interesting reading. As fixture lists varied from club to club, the table was decided on percentage as a measurement of success. It was not until 1990 that a properly structured league system was introduced in Wales, by which time many of the clubs featured in 1969 would have fallen into varying levels of decline.

Welsh Club Championship

	P.	W.	D.	L.	Points F.	A.	Av.
Newport	45	38	3	4	716	311	87.77
Cardiff	43	31	3	9	572	300	75.58
Llanelli	45	33	2	10	604	331	75.55
LdnWelsh	33	24	1	8	625	325	74.24
Abertillery	41	28	4	9	470	325	73.17
Ebbw Vale	44	30	3	11	676	333	71.59
Tredegar	28	17	4	7	340	205	67.85
Maesteg	38	24	2	12	446	274	65.78
Bridgend	45	27	5	13	679	446	65.55
Pontypridd	37	19	3	15	474	319	55.40
Neath	41	22	1	18	508	381	54.87
Newbridge	37	18	4	15	468	360	54.05
Aberavon	41	19	2	20	493	423	48.78
Swansea	42	14	3	25	472	499	36.90
Glam. W.	31	9	3	19	262	348	33.87
Cross Keys	37	10	2	25	265	488	29.72
Pontypool	47	12	2	33	367	644	27.65
Penarth	35	5	0	30	192	899	14.28

As the 1960s drew to a close Newport RFC could reflect on a decade that had produced a consistently high standard of rugby that both achieved results and entertained. A total of nineteen players represented Wales of whom B.V. Meredith, D. Watkins and B. Price were honoured with the captaincy. Six players represented the club on British Isles tours. However, it is, perhaps, for the record against the southern hemisphere touring sides that the decade will be best remembered. The sixties began with a narrow defeat by South Africa, followed by a victory over New Zealand and a drawn game with Australia. In November 1969 the Springboks were again the visitors and Newport recorded a victory to rank alongside the 1912 triumph. The Sixth Springboks' tour will be remembered more for the off the field events than the rugby. The tourists arrived amidst a wave of protest that would accompany them wherever they went during the three-month visit. Apartheid was the issue and the public were divided – rugby or politics? Most matches were targeted by the anti-apartheid protestors and the game at Newport was no exception. Before kick-off the ground was surrounded by police, with protestors and spectators trying to make their way to the turnstiles. Order was maintained and a peaceful protest did not disrupt the match. In front of a crowd of 22,000, tries by Alan Skirving and David Cornwall, together with a penalty and conversion by captain John Anthony, against two penalties by P. Visagie saw Newport through to a 11-6 win. The winning Newport XV were, from left to right, back row: P. Rose (substitute), P. Watts, D. Haines, L. Martin, J. Watkins, B. Llewellyn, G. Sutton, G. Jones (substitute). Middle row: A. Skirving, I. Taylor, V. Perrins, J. Anthony (captain), K. Poole, L. Daniels, P. Rees (substitute). Front row: W.H. Raybould, G. Treharne, A. Evans (substitute), D. Cornwall.

Alan Skirving rounds opposite number Grobler to score Newport's opening try. Jeff Watkins had won a line-out on the Springbok line and good handling by the Newport three-quarters gave Skirving his chance.

Piet Visagie manages to get his kick in despite the close attention of number eight Paul Watts, with Jeff Watkins, Del Haines, Keith Poole and Vic Perrins following up.

From the front of a line-out, Springbok G. Pitzer is about to feed scrum-half and captain Dawie de Villiers. In the centre of the line-out with the headband is Frik du Preez. In a Test career spanning 12 seasons, du Preez played 38 times for the Springboks. He made his debut against England on the 1960/61 tour and his last appearance was against Australia in 1971. At the time of writing it is suggested he will be named South Africa's Player of the Century.

In December 1968 Martin Webber, the previous year's club captain, was killed in a road accident near Banbury in Oxfordshire. He was regarded as one of the club's brightest prospects for international honours. When David Watkins completed his transfer to Rugby League club Salford, Martin Webber took over the leadership. A strong, mobile prop forward, he made 123 appearances for the club between joining in 1965/66 and his untimely death. An annual award was presented by his family – the Martin Webber Memorial Bowl is awarded to the Club Man of the Year. The first year of the award saw joint recipients in Del Haines and Keith Poole.

Three
David Watkins MBE

David Watkins first came to the attention of the rugby world while playing for Cwmcelyn Youth. Watkins captained the side in 1959/60 and also led the team, which was particularly successful in seven-a-side competitions. In fact, Cwmcelyn Youth seven-a-side team (shown here) never lost a game when Watkins played. As an introduction to senior rugby, youth players were allowed to play four games per season at the higher level before making a commitment to join a club. Watkins drew a lot of interest from the clubs in the Gwent valleys and appeared for Blaina, Abertillery, Ebbw Vale and Pontypool before making his final choice of club.

12 Commercial Street
Risca   Mon. 31. 8. 61.

Dear Mr Watkins, I have not yet met you at Newport, but doubtless will do so on Saturday. However, as David has been selected for our game against Penarth, I thought I would drop you a line so that you would know how we feel about him at Newport; no doubt the public & the newspapers will say plenty about him as well!

Your son is a truly brilliant prospect and we gave much thought after our trial on Wednesday, whether he should go into the first $\overline{XV}$ immediately, or wait. Our reasons for deciding to play him were, firstly — that though not a big chap he is fast, strong & fit, and his play bears the look of maturity. We recalled that he has played all his rugby in the top of the Western Valley, and a better testing ground than that would be hard to find.

Secondly, the power of the Newport pack is such that he will probably get more support & protection behind them & Billy Watkins, than he would in our limited $\overline{XV}$.

David Watkins wrote to Newport RFC after speaking to R.T. 'Bob' Evans. The nineteen year old was invited to take part in the club's pre-season trials and made an immediate impression. The decision was made to play him at outside-half in the opening game of the season.

Thirdly, and now I am going to be quite frank with you, the few flashes of attack we have seen from David has caught the imagination of many Newport supporters and his reception from them will, I'm sure, be most heartening.

But my last point is not the most important one at all – I just want you to know that, contrary to what many of our critics say, Newport do not play anybody regardless of their age or physique simply to draw the crowd – we have selected David because we think he is as ready now as he will ever be for first-class rugby, and because we think that fine player though Geoff Davies is, your son might well prove even better. If he doesn't, and we think a spell in our limited would help – we will advise that, & give him the best possible coaching.

You must be very proud of him!

Yours sincerely,
Bryn Williams (Chairman)

This letter was sent to Watkins's father by Bryn Williams, the chairman of Newport RFC. It clearly says what the club felt about the young player and suggests that David would be guided in a responsible way at the outset of his rugby career.

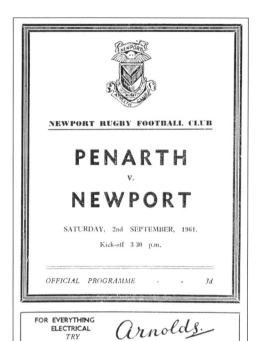

At this time, the opening game of the season was traditionally a home match against Penarth. Joining Watkins in making his first appearance for the club was back row forward Alan Thomas. Both players made try-scoring debuts and quickly established themselves in the First XV on a regular basis. It is worth recording that Watkins appeared in 39 games of the 44 played in the season with Thomas playing in every match. In his six seasons at Newport, David Watkins made 202 appearances and scored a total of 288 points, including 165 points scored from 55 drop goals. He captained the club in three consecutive seasons from 1964 to 1967 and was elected to continue in the 1967/68 season, but his decision to play Rugby League cut short his fourth term in charge.

The Newport squad in 1966/67, David Watkins' last full season with the club. From left to right, back row: G. Lewis (attendant), K. Poole, P. Watts, S.J. Watkins, B. Price, W. Morris, J. Jeffrey, J. Palmer, J. Anthony, G. Britton, A.J. Panting (match hon. secretary). Middle row: B. Perrins, A. Thomas, R.T. Carter (football hon. secretary), D. Watkins (captain), P. Hill (chairman), V. Perrins, P. Rees. Front row: M. Webber, D. Perrot, K. Jarrett, D. Cornwall.

Watkins won the first of his 21 Welsh caps against England in 1963, captaining the side in his last three games. The final match in 1967, also against England, was Keith Jarrett's debut for Wales. Waiting in the wings was Barry John, then of Llanelli, who had replaced Watkins in two internationals prior to his recall as captain. How the careers of these two fine players would have developed, if events had not taken their course, will always be a subject of conjecture. Here, referee Ernie Lewis watches as David Watkins finds a gap during the home fixture against Llanelli in 1965. Bill Morris is the Newport player behind Watkins while Llanelli's John Leleu covers.

The trophy room. A career in Rugby Union is reflected in the tankards, medals and cups on display. Although a player may represent Wales several times, he will only receive one cap. Jerseys are often exchanged but the first one is usually kept.

With all his achievements for club and country, it was certain that David Watkins would become a British Lion. Season 1966 saw the touring side visit Australia and New Zealand under the captaincy of Mike Campbell-Lamerton. Watkins appeared in all six Test matches played and was captain in the second and fourth Tests against New Zealand. Although not the most successful tour – all four Tests against the All Blacks were lost – Watkins proved a popular tourist and the rugby public down under enjoyed his adventurous and exciting approach to the game. Watkins, followed by Jim Telfer and Alun Pask, leads out the British Lions for the fourth Test against New Zealand in Auckland. Brian Loclore, the All Black captain, is ahead of Chris Laidlaw.

BRITISH ISLES RUGBY UNION TEAM
1966

Mrs. D. Watkins,   Palmerston North,
107 East Pentwyn,   New Zealand,
Blaina,
Monmouthshire,   27th July, 1966.
SOUTH WALES. U.K.

Dear Mrs Watkins,

    Now that our tour of New Zealand is more than half-way through, may I say
what a wonderful asset David has been to this party. He is probably the most
outstanding Rugby player with the team, and he has delighted the crowds in New Zealand,
but particularly in Australia, where his name will be remembered as long as rugby
is played. He is also a most cheerful, happy, and hopeful tourist, and has joined
in all the social duties asked of him.

    I feel sure that he is enjoying the tour as much as we all are now, and feels
that the days are going by fairly quickly.

        With best wishes to you all in Blaina,

                        Yours sincerely,

A short letter home from Des O'Brien assuring the family that all is well 12,000 miles away. This was a nice gesture at a time when international communication networks were not of the standard that is very much taken for granted at the start of the twenty-first century.

Wednesday 18 October 1967 saw David Watkins make his last appearance in a Newport jersey. His Union career had gone full circle, from its start at Cwmcelyn it would end just up the road at Abertillery. The following day Watkins drove up the M6 and signed for Salford Rugby League Football Club for a record fee of £15,000. He would make his debut appearance against Oldham the next night. During his time at Newport, Watkins had seen John Anderson (Huddersfield), John Mantle (St Helens) and scrum-half partners Bob Prosser (St Helens) and Cliff Williams (Hunslet) sign professional papers. Prosser later joined Watkins at Salford.

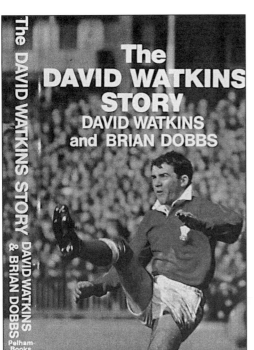

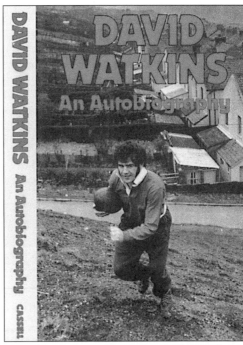

An almost obligatory part of being a sporting personality is the publication of a biography or autobiography. *The David Watkins Story* was written in collaboration with Brian Dobbs and published in 1971. After retiring in 1980, a second book, *David Watkins – An Autobiography*, appeared which brought the story up to date.

Same ball, different ground. Salford Rugby League Football Club became home to David Watkins for the best part of twelve years. In his final season (1979/80) he joined Swinton RLFC but played in only 20 games. Watkins' full League record shows that he played a total of 472 games and scored 3,117 points. Between April 1971 and April 1974 he played in a record run of 140 consecutive games, scoring in 92 consecutive games – another record. The 1973/74 season saw David Watkins kick a world record 221 goals. As in Rugby Union, Watkins achieved all the honours that League had to offer at international level. In addition to 6 appearances for Great Britain he also played for, and captained, the Welsh side 16 times.

For any Rugby League player an appearance in a Challenge Cup final is a major achievement. At the end of his second season with Salford, David Watkins led the club to it's sixth final. Only once, in 1938, had the trophy been lifted by the Salford captain and unfortunately they were to finish as runners-up again. Castleford won the Yorkshire versus Lancashire final 11-6, with Watkins confirming 'they came at us from the start and knocked us off our game – we never recovered'.

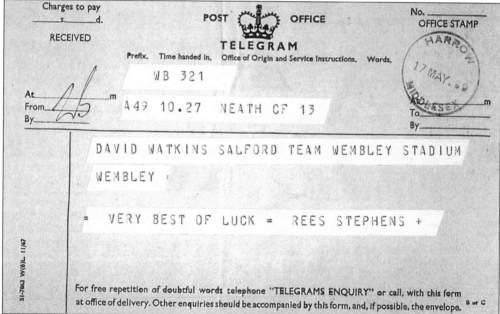

David Watkins was one of many Welsh players who joined the Rugby League code. In the majority of cases the only reason for the move was financial and by breaking away from the amateur game players had to abide by many restrictions imposed by the Union authorities. Many of those in authority took exception to what was often seen as a player's disloyalty. It must have been very gratifying for David Watkins to receive this telegram on the day of the Challenge Cup final. Rees Stephens was a member of the Welsh selectors known as 'The Big Five', who would have given Watkins his chances at international level.

In 1978 David Watkins was granted an honorary MA by Salford University and in 1986 was awarded an MBE for services to sport. He returned to Newport RFC in 1992 as team manager and in 1994 became club chairman, a position he still holds. In this photograph, taken at a dinner in recognition of David Waters' services to Newport Rugby Club, he is seen with, from left to right: Max Boyce, Brian Price, Keith Jarrett, Jim Mills, Paul Watts, David Waters, Brian Cresswell, Jeff Watkins, Campbell Black, Stuart Watkins, Gerald Davies, Del Haines.

Four

One Hundred Years Old

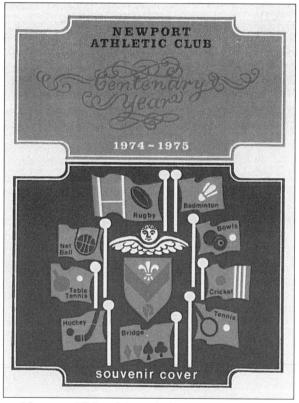

In the 1974/75 season Newport RFC celebrated their centenary. A football club had been formed in 1874 but no fixtures could be organised until a match was played in Cardiff against Glamorgan RFC on 5 April 1875, which resulted in a draw. Known originally as Newport Cricket, Athletic and Football Club the name was changed to Newport Athletic Club in 1894. The above was designed by Douglas Halliday ARCA to commemorate the club's centenary and was used on a first day cover issued on 12 September 1974.

The stamps used on the first day cover had originally been used on a 25 August 1971 cover, celebrating the centenary of the Rugby Football Union. The stamp depicts players from Cambridge University and Newport. In addition to being a member of the Welsh Rugby Union, Newport also enjoys membership of the Rugby Football Union, the only club to be affiliated to both unions.

For the centenary season Geoff Evans was invited to continue as club captain. He had led the team in 1972/73 and 1973/74 but his third term in office would be cut short. A knee injury received in the game against Tonga in October proved serious enough to confine him to the sidelines for the rest of the season. Back row colleague John Jeffery, a previous club captain, took over. Geoff Evans would captain the club again twice, in 1978/79 and 1980/81.

During its history the club had reached the heights and, indeed, sustained a remarkable level of success. The six invincible seasons and the victories over all three major touring sides from the southern hemisphere, together with the huge contribution to Welsh international rugby and British Isles touring sides, confirmed its standing in world rugby. Since the 1968/69 championship season the club's fortunes had fluctuated. Of 241 games played over 5 seasons, 133 were won, 96 lost and 12 drawn, with the highlight being the victory over South Africa. For the centenary season four special matches were arranged. A Welsh President's XV, Tonga, Crawshays and a Carwyn James International XV all visited Rodney Parade, thus ensuring many of the leading players of the day would join in the celebrations. Two dates stood out on the fixture list. While Newport were defeating Crawshays on 29 October, Muhammed Ali created boxing history by beating George Foreman in Zaire to regain the World Heavyweight Championship. On 11 February, Newport lost away to Bath and on the same day Margaret Thatcher became the first woman to lead a political party in the United Kingdom. The full results for the season show that of 50 matches played 28 were won, 18 lost and 4 drawn, with 688 points scored and 575 conceded. The cup run ended at the quarter-final stage, losing away to Bridgend 18-7. This team photograph for 1974/75 shows, from left to right, back row: J. Thomas (attendant), N. Edwards, K. Davies, J. Dale, A. Mogridge, L. Jones, J. Watkins, A. Poole, C. Smart, J. Martin, J. Ryan (coach). Middle row: R. Morgan, D. Ford, R.T. Carter (hon. secretary), G. Evans (captain), B.J. Jones (chairman), J. Jeffery, A. Williams (match secretary), P. Watts, D. Burcher. Front row: A. Evans, J. Hazzard, C. Jenkins.

Tonga's first visit to Rodney Parade was marred by the sending off of second row forward Fa'aleo Tupi late in the second half of the match for punching Newport full-back Jeff Hazzard. Newport ran out winners 14-6. In the era of the four-point try Newport scored two, by Hazzard and Ken Davies, with Hazzard also kicking two penalties. In the line-out shown here, the Newport players are, from left to right: Keith Poole, John Jeffery, Paul Watts, Jeff Watkins (jumping), Colin Smart, Ian Barnard, Jim Dale.

The first special centenary match saw the Welsh Rugby Union President XV defeat Newport 17-13. From left to right back row: O. Alexander, R. Blythe, K. Poole, M. Dowling, D. Burcher, I. Barnard, K. Davies, D. Morris. Third row: R. Burnett (touch judge), A. Mages, C. Smart, D. Hughes, J. Watkins, W. Evans, C. Owen, G. Howls, P. Watts, M. Joseph (referee), C. Black (touch judge). Second row: D. Hadden, S. Fenwick, D. Ford, A. Lewis (President XV captain), H.M. Bowcott (president of WRU), G. Evans (Newport captain), C. Rees, J. Martin, I. Hall. Front row: R. Morgan, C. Shell, A. Evans, C. Jenkins, M. Grindle, J. Hazzard.

A typical action shot of Newport right wing Ken Davies on the charge against Tonga. Ken had joined the club from Abergavenny in 1973 and was a great favourite with the Newport supporters. His aggression and pace rewarded him with many tries, including 25 in the centenary season.

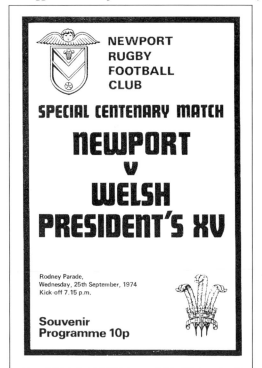

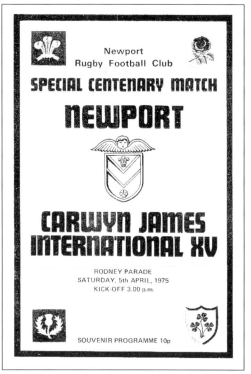

Specially designed programmes for two of the four fixtures that commemorated the centenary season.

The dust jacket of *One Hundred Years of Newport Rugby* by Jack Davies. Sadly, Davies died on 28 April 1974 and did not see his definitive work in print. He was also the author of a previous work, *Newport Rugby Football Club: 1875-1960*.

The players and officials who took part in the Newport versus Carwyn James International XV match on 5 April 1975, which was won 44-28 by the International XV. Newport player Tony Mogridge replaced Delme Thomas in the visitors' team, where he joined another ex-Newport player John Uzzell and future Newport coach A.G. 'Charlie' Faulkner. From left to right, back row: B. Lease, A. Faulkner, D. Burcher, J. James, P. Watts, T. David, D. Wilson, P. Tikoisuva. Third row: R. Morgan, L. Baxter, L. Jones, A. Mogridge, S. Willis, D. Hughes, J. Watkins, G.J.R. Thomas, C. Smart, R. Windsor, D. Ford, D.M. Lloyd (referee), C. Black (touch judge). Second row: T. O'Gorman, J. Uzzell, R.T. Carter (hon. secretary), J. Jeffery (Newport captain), B.J. Jones (chairman), Carwyn James, G.O. Edwards (Invitation XV captain), I. Williams (match secretary), P. Bennett, J. Martin, J. Spencer. Front row: J. Hazzard, J.J. Williams A. Evans, R. Davies, R. Burnett (touch judge).

The centenary celebrations were formally wound up at a banquet held at the Rodney Hall on 16 May 1975. A lot of water had flowed under the Newport bridge since the early days saw rugby first played on the other side of the Usk at the Marshes, now Shaftesbury Park. In 100 years Newport had played 3,270 matches, of which 2,200 were won, 767 lost and 303 drawn. A total of 54 players had been honoured with the captaincy of the club.

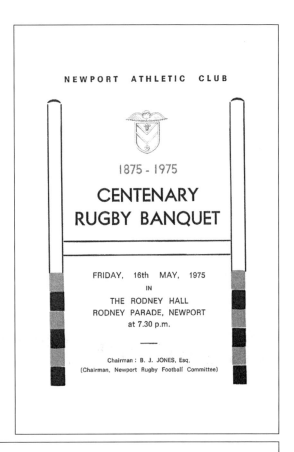

NEWPORT ATHLETIC CLUB

1875 - 1975

CENTENARY RUGBY BANQUET

FRIDAY, 16th MAY, 1975
IN
THE RODNEY HALL
RODNEY PARADE, NEWPORT
at 7.30 p.m.

Chairman : B. J. JONES, Esq.
(Chairman, Newport Rugby Football Committee)

MENU

Minestrone Soup
——
Sole Veronique
——
Roast Beef
Horseradish Sauce
——
Roast and Boiled Potatoes
Broccoli Spears au Gratin
Creamed Carrots
——
Sherry Trifle
——
Assorted Cheeses
Coffee
——
Acknowledgement—
The wines were generously provided by
Courage (Western) Ltd.

All catering arrangements carried out by
R. H. Stevens & Sons, Abergavenny

TOAST LIST

Grace
will be said by F. W. HARRISON, Esq.,
President, Newport Athletic Club

The Queen
Mr. B. J. JONES,
Chairman, Newport Rugby Football Club

The Newport Rugby Club
Proposed by   -   HUW WHELDON, Esq.,
Managing Director, B.B.C. Television.
Response by   -   Mr. B. J. JONES,
Chairman, Newport Rugby Football Club.
Newport—Barbarians—Wales.

Our Guests
Proposed by   -   Mr. R. T. EVANS,
Newport Rugby Football Committee.
Newport—Wales—British Lions.
Response by   -   CLIFF MORGAN, Esq.,
Head of Outside Broadcasts, B.B.C.
Radio.
Cardiff—Barbarians—Wales—British
Lions.

Toastmaster   -   -   Mr. GODFREY PAGE

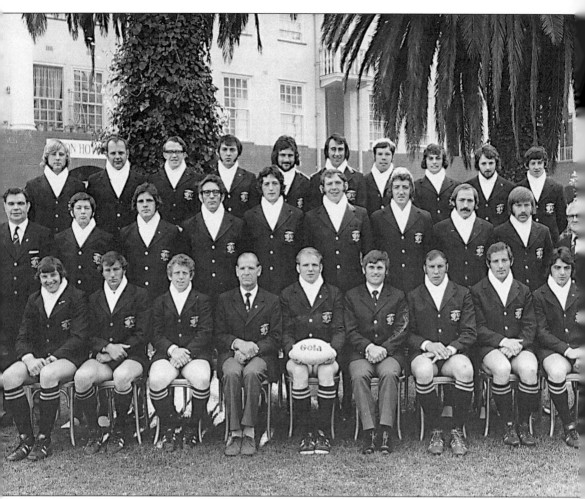

When Reg Skrimshire toured South Africa with the British Isles team in 1903 this started an association between Newport RFC and South African rugby that holds strong to this day. A Newport player and later club chairman, J.E.C. 'Bird' Partridge gained a cap for South Africa against the 1903 tourists and Newport's games against touring Springboks are well reported. It was not surprising that Newport should accept an invitation from the Northern Transvaal Rugby Union to tour South Africa in 1973. On the back of a disappointing season, guest players were invited to join the party, including Dennis Hughes and Tony Browning of Newbridge, Ken Plummer of Bristol and Aberavon's Ian Hall. The opposition proved far too strong, however, and all 6 matches were lost. The tour party included, from left to right, back row: P. Williams, I. Barnard, B. Phillips, G. Williams, P. Ward, K. Plummer, I. Hall, L. Thomas, T. Browning, V. Jenkins. Middle row: R.T. Evans, R. Williams, J. Dale, D. Hughes, T. Mogridge, L. Jones, J. Watkins, D. Haines, B. Rowland, M. Dawes. Front row: G. Fuller, K. Poole, A. Evans, A. Panting (manager), G. Evans (captain), B. Jones (coach), P. Watts, P. Williams, L. Davies.

BIRTHDAY GREETINGS AND CONGRATULATIONS
from the South African Rugby Football Union, Capetown

On behalf of the South African Rugby Board and all rugby followers of my country, we wish to extend to the Newport Rugby Club our congratulations on this milestone they have reached in their history and all wish them well for the next hundred years.

Newport, to all South Africans, has become a household word. Firstly, because of the very hard games our Springboks always have had against this famous Club, for the narrow victories we have celebrated and even for the defeat which cost us our Springbok head. We, therefore, have the greatest respect and admiration for this Club.

The second reason why we honour it, is because of the great personalities your Club has given to the rugby world. I know that these personalities will be dealt with in your brochures or books, but I would like to mention one who meant so much because of his rugby wisdom to me and to many Springbok teams, namely Tommy Vile, who not only was a grand player, an outstanding referee, but an outstanding man.

We also honour the Newport Rugby Club because of its contribution towards the evolution of this game. We realise that rugby would have been poorer if it was not for this contribution, and we believe that contributions do not cease when a Club is dynamic as Newport has always been.

We are also proud of the fact that we have had more associations with Newport than the mere playing of matches. Several of your players have come to this country and have played for some of our teams. It is perhaps not known, but one of your players, Lt. J. E. C. Partridge, after the Anglo Boer war, remained here for a while, and shortly after the smoke of cannons and rifles had cleared up in that war, played for South Africa, and as such, became one of our Springboks. This is the spirit of rugby— notwithstanding wars, rugby relationships stand out and everything is forgotten when it comes to this wonderful game.

Thanks, Newport, for everything, but thanks also for giving us the Springbok, who helped to lay the foundations of the game in this country and of our attitude towards the game, the countries in which it is played and the clubs in those countries.

Dr. Danie H. Craven
President S.A.R.F.U.

During the centenary season, letters of congratulations were received from all parts of the rugby world. Many of these were reproduced in the programmes, including this one which was received from Danie Craven, president of the South African RFU.

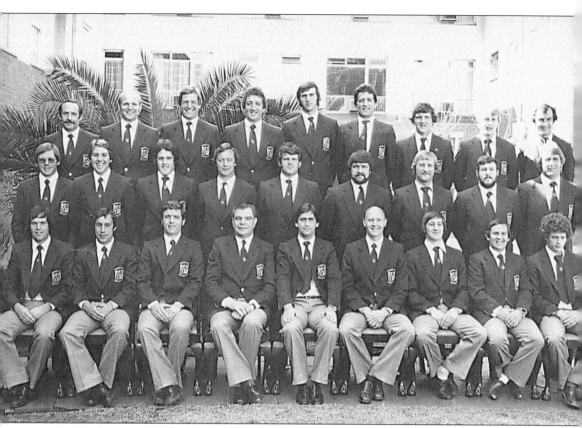

A second tour to South Africa followed in 1979. Of six games played, five were lost with an 18-18 draw against a SA Rugby Press Association XV at Port Elizabeth. Although they did not win a game, Newport proved much stronger opponents than their predecessors had in 1973. Narrow defeats against South African Colleges (10-13) and Northern Transvaal Under-25s (20-23), both at Pretoria, and 16-19 against Eastern Province at Port Elizabeth were a marked improvement. It was only against a Far North XV (18-30) at Pietersburg and Western Transvaal (22-38) at Potchestroom that Newport were well beaten. Against Western Transvaal, Newport second row Jeff Watkins made his 350th appearance for the club and celebrated by scoring one of his side's four tries. Notable among the Western Province XV was Andre Markgraaf, who would later coach the Springboks and subsequently resign under very political circumstances. The 1979 tour party comprised, from left to right, back row: D. Burcher, G. Evans, R. Barrell, J. Watkins, D. Waters, A. Mogridge, K. Davies, D. Cornwall, R. Powell. Middle row: J. Cranton, C. Webber, J. Churchill, P. Waters, M. Othen, D. Jones, P. Williams, R. Morgan, M. McJennett. Front row: D. Barry, A. Billinghurst, S. O'Donoghue, R.T. Evans (manager), G. Evans (captain), S. Jeffreys (coach), R. Clifford, L. Davies, J. Robinson.

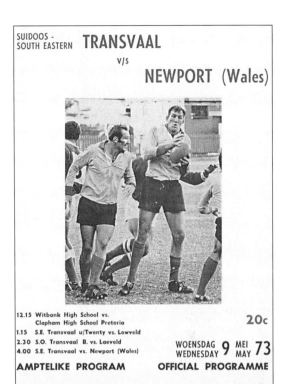

A selection of programmes from the 1973 and 1979 tours to South Africa. Programmes are very popular with collectors of rugby memorabilia. Those for games overseas are particularly sought-after items.

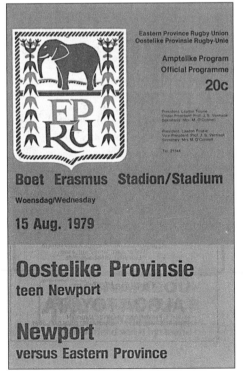

Although Newport visited South Africa twice in the 1970s, it would be twenty-five years before the Springboks returned to the UK following the 1969/70 tour. Political pressure forced South African sport into isolation and they spent many years without experiencing international competition. When the sanctions were eventually lifted, the rugby world had changed and the days of the long overseas tour had changed for good. New Zealand and Australia continued extensive overseas tours into the 1980s, but at the start of the twenty-first century it appears very unlikely that clubs such as Newport will have the opportunity to play major sides from the southern hemisphere again. The modern tour is short, totally focused on international rugby and with few midweek matches. Those played are usually against regional or combined XVs. In 1973, however, New Zealand visited Rodney Parade and played a Newport side given very little chance of causing the tourists any problems. In losing 15-20 Newport gave the All Blacks a real scare. At half time Newport were very much in the game at 6-6 but two contentious penalty decisions by referee Air Commodore Larry Lamb took the game away from the home side. The game also saw Lynn Jones and Peter Whiting forget the mood of the 1960s and proceed to make war not love even if, from the terraces, it looked the other way around! This photograph of the Newport team shows, from left to right, back row: B. Rowland, I. Barnard, L. Jones, J. Watkins, J. Jeffery, P. Watts. Middle row: N. Edwards, A. Evans, G. Evans (captain), G. Fuller, R. Williams. Front row: D. Rogers, G. Talbot, G. Williams, P. Ward.

The 1975/76 season was the club's most successful for seven years. Under the captaincy of Colin Smart, Newport scored a total of 1,079 points – the first time the 1,000-point barrier had been broken. The touring Australians were the first side to win at Rodney Parade in the season. A comparatively small crowd of 12,000 saw Newport beaten 7-13 in a match they started as favourites. It was not Newport's day as missed goal kicks and general poor play compounded a performance that is best forgotten. Memories of the drawn match in 1966 drew comparisons and two golden opportunities to defeat a major touring side were missed.

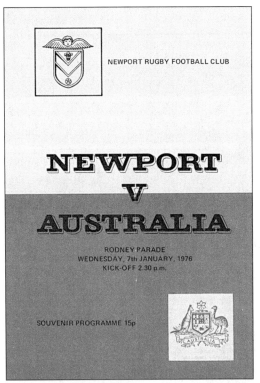

NEWPORT RUGBY FOOTBALL CLUB

NEWPORT
V
AUSTRALIA

RODNEY PARADE
WEDNESDAY, 7th JANUARY, 1976
KICK-OFF 2.30 p.m.

SOUVENIR PROGRAMME 15p

During 1975/76 only 3 home games were lost while in the following season an unbeaten home record was maintained. The second side to win at Rodney Parade in 1975/76 was Llanelli in the quarter-final of the WRU Challenge Cup; Newport were comprehensively beaten 4-21. In this photograph, scrum-half Allan Evans passes to David Rogers. Derek Quinnell and Hefin Jenkins are the Llanelli players on the right. The only other side to go away with a win was Aberavon, who won the last match of the season 25-9. Newport were runners up in the Welsh Championship, losing out to Pontypridd. They were second again in the following season when Llanelli got the silverware.

Season 1971/72 saw the reintroduction of the Welsh Rugby Union Challenge Cup. Cup competitions were first introduced in the late nineteenth century. Newport were very successful in the earlier tournaments, running out winners on five occasions. In 1972 the new tournament gained support from all quarters. The promise of an appearance in a final at Cardiff Arms Park held great appeal to the players and the junior clubs had a chance to play the 'big boys' and, indeed, produce the occasional upset. For the first five seasons Llanelli dominated the tournament – they were runners-up in the first final and winners of the next four. Newport had not progressed beyond the quarter-final stage but in 1976/77 they went all the way. Early round victories at home against Resolven 80-0, and Neyland 44-4 were followed by a 12-12 draw at Tumble, with Newport progressing on the try count rule. Club captain David Burcher scored the try that took the club to a quarter-final away to Newbridge. A 13-10 victory saw Newport through to a semi-final against Ebbw Vale in Cardiff. A controversial tackle by Newport wing Jeff Cranton on Ebbw Vale full-back Peter Griffiths stole the headlines. Griffiths was concussed and took no further part in the match, which saw a David Rogers try and Leighton Davies penalty gain a 7-3 win and a place in the final. Centenary celebrating Cardiff were the other finalists and, like Newport, had to rely on the try count ruling to take them past the quarter-final stage. Two tries scored in a 10-10 draw at Pontypool got Cardiff through to a semi-final against Aberavon at Swansea. This game was won 15-6 and the stage was set for a classic Newport-Cardiff encounter. The 1976/77 Challenge Cup winners, from left to right, back row: S. Jeffries (coach), R. Barrell, K. Davies, I. Barnard, J. Watkins, D. Waters, J. Squire, C. Webber, J. Cranton, J. Ryan (coach). Middle row: R. Morgan, D. Ford, D. Rogers, R.T. Carter (hon. secretary), C. Smart (captain), R. Atkins (chairman), N. Brown, A. Williams (match secretary), L. Davies. Front row: F. Headon, T. O'Gorman, S. Phillips, H. Davies, A. Billinghurst, B. Lease.

The British Isles party to tour New Zealand was announced and two Newport players, club captain David Burcher and Gareth Evans, had been selected. Both reluctantly chose to stand down from the final, in case of injury. Cardiff had only one representative in the tour party, scrum-half Brynmor Williams, but with G.O. Edwards as first choice Cardiff had no problems in this position. Gerald Davies on the wing and a wealth of experience in the forwards saw Cardiff start the match as favourites. Newport were forced to make one change on the morning of the game. Hooker Steve Jones had received burns from a sun lamp and David Ford took over. Neil Brown and Chris Webber stood in for Burcher and Evans while veterans Keith Poole and Ian Barnard were chosen and played major roles. One of the best finals saw Newport win 16-15. Tries by wings Davies and Cranton, a Leighton Davies penalty and a penalty and conversion by Chris Webber gave Newport a well-deserved victory. Ian Barnard won the Lloyd Lewis Memorial Trophy awarded to the man of the match and Colin Smart, leading the side in Burcher's absence, received the cup.

Twelve months later Newport had the chance to retain the trophy but were not able to raise their game. A crowd of 40,000 witnessed a disappointing final, which Swansea won 13-9. Whatever the sport, cup competitions are always likely to produce giant-killing acts and Newport RFC can certainly bear witness to this. The first round of the 1980/81 tournament saw Newport drawn away to Penclawydd. In gale force conditions Newport gifted an early try from a charge down and were never able to recover, losing 4-0. In 1993/94 it was the turn of Ystradgynlais to humble the Usksiders. Newport old boy Mike Lewis controlled the game and scored 5 points in his side's 10-9 victory.

Newport scrum-half Alan Billinghurst gets his pass away to outside-half David Rogers in the 1977 Cup Final. Cardiff hooker Alan Phillips is moving in on Rogers while Ian Barnard (top left), Gareth Edwards and David Ford (on the ground) look on.

Newport's only cup victory to date was duly celebrated in appropriate style. Richard Barrell and Rhys Morgan led the singing in the communal bath.

Right: Invited to join the Welsh squad in 1974, Colin Smart declined, preferring to push towards an international career with England. Smart was duly rewarded in 1979 when he won the first of his 17 caps in a victory over France and was in the England team that defeated Australia in 1982. This was the day that rugby took a back seat and Erica Roe stole the headlines. In the April 1982 edition of *Rugby World* a player profile of Colin was published. Among his answers he named his most difficult opponents as the Newport committee, his favourite ground as Rodney Parade and his rugby ambition, 'to play with the topless streaker at Twickenham'! Colin Smart played 291 games for Newport and captained the club in seasons 1975/76 and 1982/83.

Left: Prior to the Second World War, Newport had supplied four players to the cause of English rugby: R. Dibble, R. Edwards, E.D.G. Hammett and S.H. Williams. Post-war – in addition to Colin Smart – Jack Hancock, a second row forward, played twice for England in 1955. Later that year Hancock became another player lost to the Northern League. This time Salford got their man and over the next five seasons Jack Hancock played 104 games for the club before retiring in November 1960.

When the British Isles toured Australia and New Zealand in 1971 it was noticeable that no Newport player was included in the squad. Again, in 1974, when the tourists visited South Africa, Newport were not represented. Throughout the twentieth century the club had supplied players on every tour, but missed out sharing in the great successes achieved by the 1971 and 1974 sides. The announcement of the 1977 tourists included a record fifteen representatives from Wales. Among the squad were Newport captain David Burcher and fellow centre Gareth Evans. Shortly before departure they were joined by Jeff Squire, who was called up to replace Roger Uttley. Burcher and Evans were both products of Newport High School. Burcher arrived at Newport after finishing his studies at St Luke's College, Exeter, while Evans's rugby career started with Cross Keys before he joined the club. Burcher's 4 Welsh caps all came in the Five Nations matches in 1977, which saw Wales win the Triple Crown. Wales scored one of the tries of the season at Murrayfield when Burcher's overhead pass to Fenwick in the build-up was cleverly delivered. When selected to tour with the British side, Gareth Evans had only made just a single appearance for Wales – as a replacement against France in 1977. He gained a further 2 caps in 1978: against France and then in the second Test in Australia, again as a replacement. Although Newport product Robert Ackerman toured New Zealand in 1983, by then he was a London Welsh player and it is sad to relate that on the five British Isles tours since 1977 Newport has not been represented.

Jeff Squire made two further overseas tours with the British Isles, to South Africa in 1980 and New Zealand in 1983. By now, however, he was a Pontypool player, having moved from Newport in 1978. Most of his 29 caps for Wales were won while he was at Pontypool, including the 5 games in which he was Welsh captain.

Brynmor Williams joined Newport from rivals Cardiff in December 1977. He was an outstanding scrum-half who had played understudy to Gareth Edwards at Cardiff, which limited his appearances. First capped for Wales in Australia in 1978, Williams won a further 2 caps in 1981 but by this time he had moved west and was playing his rugby at Swansea. As an uncapped player he toured New Zealand with the British Isles in 1977, playing 3 Test matches.

This was taken at a Cardiff-Newport match at the Arms Park in 1972. Cardiff had moved to the new ground adjacent to the National Stadium in October 1970. Although having a capacity of 15,000, times were changing as the gaps in the stand and on the terracing show. An excellent study of a line-out, the photograph shows the players preparing to compete for the ball. The players in view are Phillips, Watkins, Evans and Poole for Newport and Beard, Robinson, Kallenos, Lane, John and Smith for Cardiff.

Five

To the Brink

```
NEWPORT (BLACK & AMBER)  6        .V.        NEATH (ALL BLACK)  12

              TO-DAY'S REFEREE ... G.M. CHALLENGER (PORTH)

15  Leighton Davies PL      Full Back        H. Beven  J.DAVIES

14  David Bale              Right Wing       D. Davies 6 LEWIS
13  Phil Waters             Right Centre     D. Cole (Capt.) J.DAVIES
12  David Rogers (CAPT)     Left Centre      C. Thomas
11  Robert Ackerman         Left Wing        B. Taylor LPC

10  Keith James >6          Outside Half     I. Rees T.C
 9  Alun Billinghurst       Inside Half      C. Ghojek


 1  Jim Dale                Forwards         R. Ratty
 2  Peter Nowell                             M. Richards (CAPT)
 3  Roy Cridland                             D. Mills
 4  David Bidgood                            P. Rawlings
 5  David Waters                             R. Hughes
 6  Geoff Evans                              G. Thomas
 8  Richard Barrell                          C. Jones
 7  Tony Aubin                               P. Pugh J.RANDALL


                            Substitutes

    Lyndon Faulkner                          G. Lewis
    David Cornwall                           S. Dando


This evening, we extend a very warm welcome to Neath and thank them for
their excellent co-operation in agreeing to play this postponed game.  We
apologise that due to the continued Printers strike, we are unable to pro-
duce our usual Match Programme.

Tonight, Members and Supporters have the opportunity of saying thankyou to
David Rogers for his magnificent contribution to Newport R.F.C. over the
last two decades, as he plays his final game before retiring.  Everyone at
Rodney Parade says "Thankyou" for your contribution on the field and are
confident it will continue in the future off the field.  "All best wishes
for the future David".

The Chairman, Captain, Committee and Players would like to thank those
loyal members and supporters for the excellent way they have stuck with the
Club through 'Their Darkest Hours'.  During the summer months ahead, a grea
deal of hard work will be needed to ensure that Newport R.F.C. can rise lik
a pheonix from the ashes.

Please note that the postponed Newport School 7 - a - side Tournament will
take place at Rodney Parade on Friday next, 2nd May, K.O. 6.00 p.m.

This evening we welcome Mr. Alun Pask and a school party from Rouen who ar
visiting the area.  We hope their stay will be a pleasant one and to-night
game one of the highlights of their visit.

PLEASE DO NOT FORGET THE CLUB'S OPEN DAY ON MONDAY, 5th MAY, 1980.
```

The programme for the final match of the 1979/80 season. A printers' strike prevented the normal publication being produced but in the brief notes that appeared, room was found to refer to 'Their Darkest Hours'. Looking at the Newport team it is difficult to believe that the season was the worst in the club's history with 33 defeats.

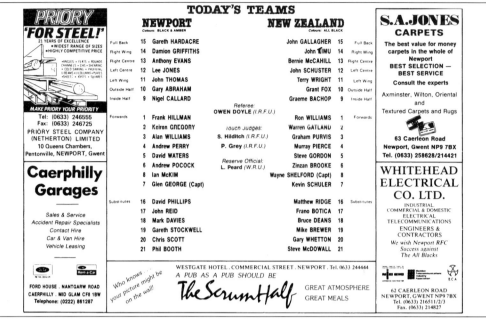

TODAY'S TEAMS

		NEWPORT		NEW ZEALAND		
		Colours: BLACK & AMBER		*Colours: ALL BLACK*		
Full Back	15	Gareth HARDACRE	John GALLAGHER	15	Full Back
Right Wing	14	Damion GRIFFITHS	John KIRWAN	14	Right Wing
Right Centre	13	Anthony EVANS	Bernie McCAHILL	13	Right Centre
Left Centre	12	Lee JONES	John SCHUSTER	12	Left Centre
Left Wing	11	John THOMAS	Terry WRIGHT	11	Left Wing
Outside Half	10	Gary ABRAHAM	Grant FOX	10	Outside Half
Inside Half	9	Nigel CALLARD	Graeme BACHOP	9	Inside Half

Referee:
OWEN DOYLE (I.R.F.U.)

Forwards	1	Frank HILLMAN		Ron WILLIAMS	1	Forwards
	2	Keiron GREGORY	*Touch Judges:*	Warren GATLAND	2	
	3	Alan WILLIAMS	S. Hilditch (I.R.F.U.)	Graham PURVIS	3	
	4	Andrew PERRY	P. Grey (I.R.F.U.)	Murray PIERCE	4	
	5	David WATERS		Steve GORDON	5	
	6	Andrew POCOCK	*Reserve Official:*	Zinzan BROOKE	6	
	7	Glen GEORGE (Capt)	L. Peard (W.R.U.)	Wayne SHELFORD (Capt)	8	
	8	Ian McKIM		Kevin SCHULER	7	

Substitutes	16	David PHILLIPS		Matthew RIDGE	16	Substitutes
	17	John REID		Frano BOTICA	17	
	18	Mark DAVIES		Bruce DEANS	18	
	19	Gareth STOCKWELL		Mike BREWER	19	
	20	Chris SCOTT		Gary WHETTON	20	
	21	Phil BOOTH		Steve McDOWALL	21	

The centenary of the WRU was celebrated in 1980/81. Special matches were arranged and one of the highlights of the season was a short tour by New Zealand. Traditionally, Cardiff, Llanelli, Newport and Swansea played major overseas touring sides and, in addition to the international, these four were given fixtures in the five-match tour. Newport played New Zealand on 28 October in the fourth match of the tour. Cardiff (16-9), Llanelli (16-10) and Swansea (32-0) had all been beaten and Newport were not expected to do any better. A crowd of 20,000 saw the visitors win 14-3 but Newport raised their game under Geoff Evans and could hold their heads up at the end of the match.

Four days later Wales were overwhelmed 3-23, their biggest home defeat for ninety-eight years. The game saw nineteen-year-old Robert Ackerman make an impressive debut. Two weeks earlier he had entered the record books by scoring six tries against Gloucester at Rodney Parade. Ackerman went on to win a total of 22 Welsh caps and in 1983, while playing at London Welsh, was a member of the British Isles team that toured New Zealand. This photograph, taken at Rodney Parade in 1981, shows Cardiff wing Steve Evans with the ball and Robert Ackerman preparing to tackle him.

The Newport First XV squad, 1980/81. From left to right, back row: C. Black (hon. match secretary), J. Robinson, D. Llewellyn, J. Dale, J. Manders, D. Waters, K. Williams, J. Churchill, Bolland, N. Webb, Adrian Hearn (hon. coach). Middle row: J. Robinson, R. Powell, R. Ackerman, P. Rees R.T. Carter (football hon. secretary), Geoff Evans (captain), B.V. Williams (chairman), G. Evans, S. O'Donoghue, R. Morgan, N. Hughes. Front row: K. James, L. Davies, G. Powell, A. Billinghurst.

The 1980 New Zealand tourists. From left to right, back row: G. Old, M. Mexted, F. Oliver, A. Haden, G. Higginson, G. Hines, M. Shaw. Third row: S. Wilson, R. Ketels, B. Robertson, J. Ashworth, G. Knight, B. Codlin, J. Spiers. Second row: M. Hood (physiotherapist), M. Donaldson, B. Fraser, M. Taylor, N. Allen, F. Woodman, D. Loveridge. Front row: R. Harper (manager), D. Rollerson, H. Reid, G. Mourie (captain), B. Osborne, A. Dalton, E. Watson (coach).

Remember those photographs of club games in the 1950s and 1960s? The terraces and stands were always well populated, particularly so when Newport played Cardiff. This photograph shows Colin Smart about to fall on the ball while Bob Lakin of Cardiff looks poised to kick it. This match took place at Rodney Parade in October 1982 and what is particularly apparent is the crowd – or the lack of it. Although Newport were experiencing difficult times in the early 1980s, a Newport-Cardiff encounter would normally expect to attract a good turnout. This was the start of a problem that the game would experience at club level to the end of the century.

Keith James relieves the pressure in the 1980 WRU Challenge Cup semi-final defeat by Swansea at Cardiff. Newport lost the game 13-23 with Keith contributing two drop goals. James joined Newport in season 1971/72, when he scored 20 drop goals, beating David Watkins' previous record of 14. He moved to Cardiff the following season, replacing the retired Barry John, but returned to Newport in 1977 after spells at Abertillery, Pontypool and a short period of club rugby in Italy. His last season at Newport was 1986/87, by which time he had scored over 100 drop goals for the club.

Mike 'Spike' Watkins joined Newport from Cardiff in 1981. In a chequered career Watkins was club captain in four consecutive seasons, from 1983 to 1987. Together with coach Charlie Faulkner, he helped Newport put together a pack of forwards that were the foundation in the reversal of the downward trend of the previous seasons. Under Watkins' captaincy, Newport won 104 of the 167 games played, a marked improvement on the previous four seasons, which had seen only 69 victories in 178 outings. Mike Watkins was one of a handful of players who captained Wales on their debut. He led the national side to victory in Ireland and won a further 3 caps, all as captain.

The 1983/84 squad that began the turnaround in the club's fortunes. From left to right, back row: C. Black (hon. match secretary), A. Faulkner (coach), A. Billinghurst, P. Steele, C. Wood, W. Rendall, D. Waters, J. Widdecombe, R. Collins, J. Rawlins, A. Coombs, D. Hall, R. Duggan (assistant coach). Front row: A. Phillips, C. Williams, R. Powell, B.J. Jones (chairman), M. Watkins (captain), D. Ackerman (hon. secretary), J. Robinson, M. Batten, P. Blight.

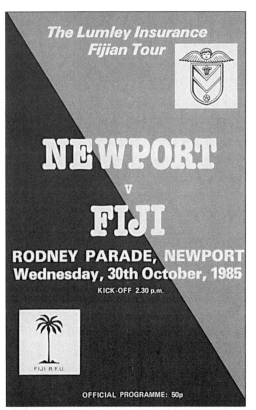

The Lumley Insurance
Fijian Tour

NEWPORT
v
FIJI

RODNEY PARADE, NEWPORT
Wednesday, 30th October, 1985

KICK-OFF 2.30 p.m.

FIJI R.F.U.

OFFICIAL PROGRAMME: 50p

For Newport RFC, 30 October is a date that is well remembered. In 1963 the All Blacks were beaten on 30 October but twenty-two years later Fiji, on their first visit to Rodney Parade, were the victors by 7-6. Only 7,500 spectators turned out to witness a dour game marred by general ill temper and the sending off of the Fijian second row Iratia Savai. Memories of another visit by South Sea islanders came to mind – in 1974 Tonga had also had a player dismissed at Newport.

Where's the ball? Rawlins, Waters and Penny look bemused as referee Mr Jones calls a halt to proceedings.

Fijian outside-half Acura Niuqila slips past Paul Daniel. Dismissed forward Savai is to the left, wearing the headband.

In an admirable gesture, committee members and administrators joined the 1984/85 squad for this photograph. From left to right, back row: M. Brown, B. Williams, D. Hill, R. Burnett, J. McCready, C. Black, C. Saunders, H. Rowland, R. Taylor, D. Rogers, J. Llewellyn, H. Mainwaring, R. Atkins. Third row: I. Barnard, A. Faulkner (coach), P. Dowdswell (trainer), D. Pitt, J. White, S. McWilliams, R. Collins, A. Perry, W. Rendall, G. George, J. Rawlins, T. Coombs, J. Watkins, R. Duggan (coach). Second row: J. Widdicombe, G. Evans, D. Waters, D. Ackerman, M.J. Watkins (captain), B.J. Jones, R. Morgan, R.T. Evans, R. Powell. Front row: H. Ali, C. Jonathan, A. Parry, S. Pill, J. Callard, P. Smith.

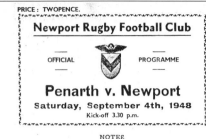

PRICE : TWOPENCE.

Newport Rugby Football Club

OFFICIAL   PROGRAMME

Penarth v. Newport

Saturday, September 4th, 1948

Kick-off 3.30 p.m.

NOTES

Penarth, almost by privilege of right, and certainly of custom, open the 1948-9 season at Rodney Parade to-day. The first game is ever the occasion of optimism and high hopes, fondly nurtured by every Club team, official and supporter in the Kingdom, that this opening match is going to indicate a side of talent and a successful season ahead. Whether or not these hopes are ever realised (and for so many they are soon to be tempered and often almost submerged under difficulties) nothing during a season's play can quite replace that anticipatory thrill of optimism that heralds, with new ball on green, unworn turf, the start of Rugby football.

To Hedley Rowland and his Newport side—our loyal support and best wishes for a successful and, may we add, an inspired season. And to Penarth—ever resolute, capable opponents—a wish similar in sincerity and purpose. And to our own supporters and Rugby followers everywhere—may the season ahead provide an ascending quality of football, with the spirit of enterprise fully in evidence.

The three Newport sides—Firsts, United and Extras—take the field to-day, and those who advocate a later start to the season will direct their sympathies to the Selection Committee, whose task it is to weld the abundance of old and new talent, following the brief and limited observation which the opening trial matches provide. Whilst the composition of the Newport Team for to-day's opening game is undecided when these notes go to Press, perhaps the outstanding item of interest, arising from the trials, is the decision of W. H. Travers to resume playing after two years of retirement. If this grand forward can—if only for a brief season or two—resume in his old form, then his play and general influence may well mould a great Newport pack—the first essential to a team of greatness. Hedley Rowland (resuming at centre three-quarter) will be readily eager to grasp the significance of this and of Travers's decision.

Quality is Sound Economy

ROATH FURNISHING CO.

137a COMMERCIAL ST., NEWPORT.   Tel. 5132.

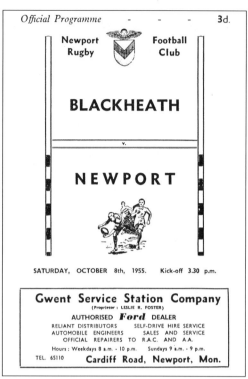

Official Programme - - - 3d.

Newport Rugby   Football Club

BLACKHEATH

v.

NEWPORT

SATURDAY, OCTOBER 8th, 1955.   Kick-off 3.30 p.m.

The post-war evolution of the Newport programme is well illustrated on these two pages. The 1948 programme was priced at twopence and contained eight pages, while in 2000 a glossy

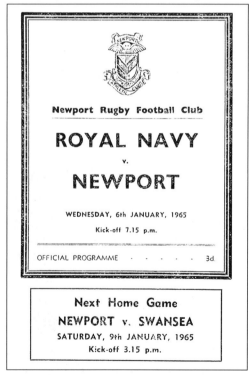

Newport Rugby Football Club

ROYAL NAVY

v.

NEWPORT

WEDNESDAY, 6th JANUARY, 1965

Kick-off 7.15 p.m.

OFFICIAL PROGRAMME - - - - - 3d.

Next Home Game
NEWPORT v. SWANSEA
SATURDAY, 9th JANUARY, 1965
Kick-off 3.15 p.m.

Newport
Rugby
Football
Club

OFFICIAL
PROGRAMME
3p

MOSELEY
VERSUS
NEWPORT

WEDNESDAY, 8th SEPTEMBER, 1971
kick-off 7.15 p.m.

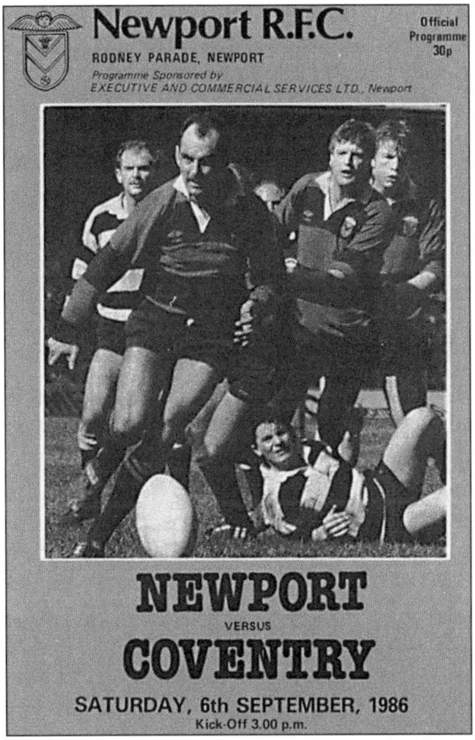

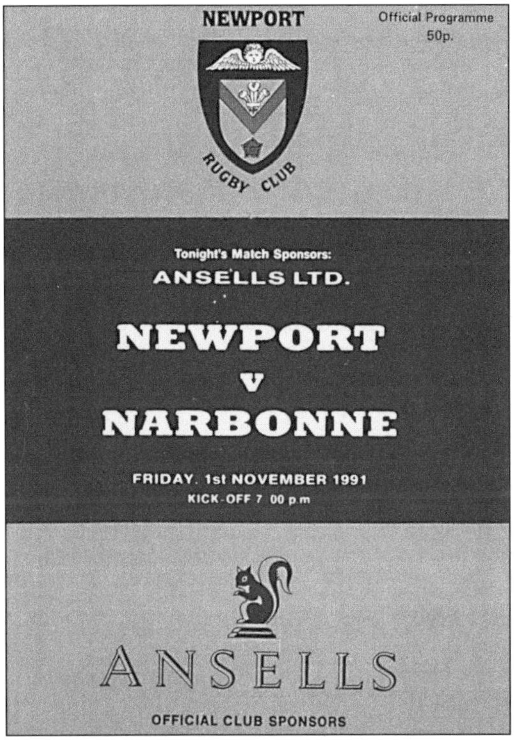

thirty-six-page production costs £1.50. (One more sentence). Kick-off times have also changed with television now calling the tune on a lot of occasions.

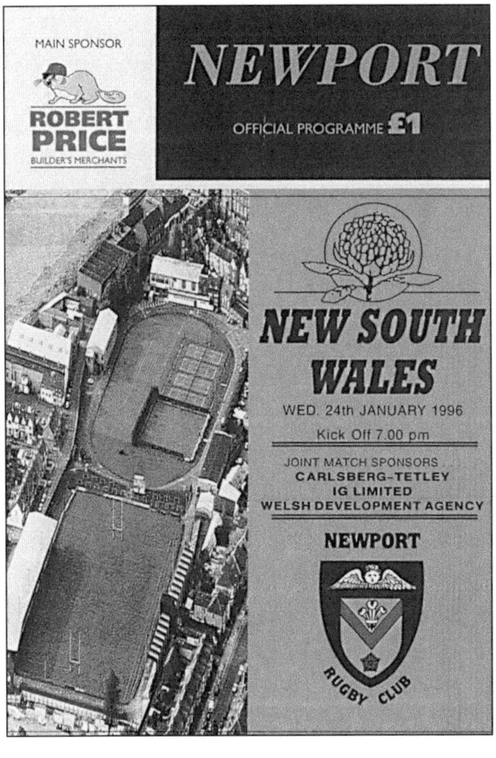

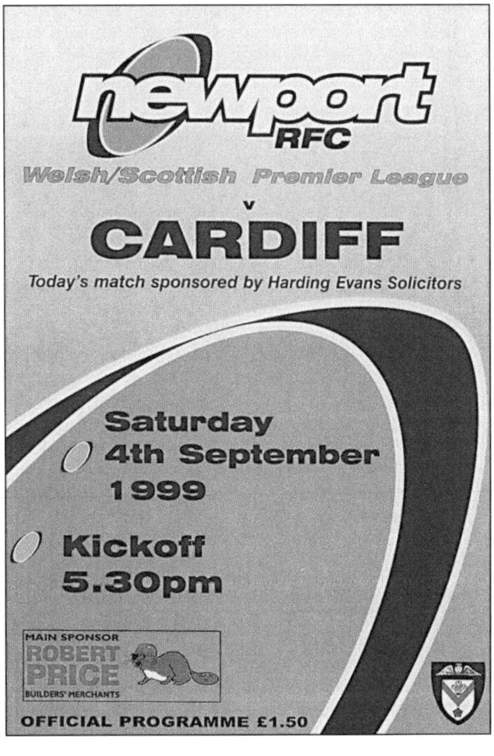

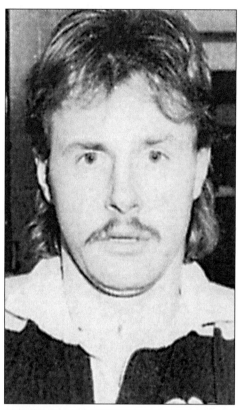

Paul Turner joined Newport from Newbridge in 1985 and made an immediate impact. In his first season with the club he scored 191 points but the following season saw him amass a record-breaking 368 points. This broke the previous best of 305 points scored by Laurie Daniel in 1971/72. Paul also holds the record for Newbridge with 405 points scored in 1983/84. Indeed, he returned to Newbridge in 1988 for their centenary season but arrived back at Newport the following year. He gained 3 Welsh caps, all in 1988/89 while a Newbridge player, and left Newport in 1992 to join Sale as player-coach.

Despite the attentions of Llanelli captain Phil Davies, Newport wing forward Glen George scores a try at Rodney Parade in March 1988. Glen George took over the captaincy in 1988/89 and held it for a record-equalling five consecutive seasons. Will Phillips was the previous player to achieve this feat in consecutive seasons (from 1877 to 1882) while, more recently, Geoff Evans led the club five times but not over consecutive years. As a result of his tireless efforts at club level, Glen was awarded due recognition in 1991 with 2 Welsh caps, against England and Scotland.

With a powerful pack of forwards and guided behind the scrum by Paul Turner, Newport reached the final of what had become the Schweppes Cup in 1986. This was the club's third appearance in a final and for the second time the opponents were Cardiff. In the four rounds leading to the semi-final Newport had enjoyed home advantage and defeated Abertillery (28-8), Mountain Ash (35-12), Wrexham (29-0) and Swansea (10-4). In the semi-final Aberavon were beaten 15-6 in Cardiff.

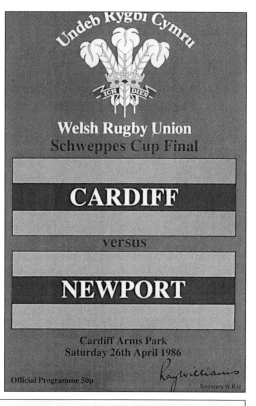

Undeb Rygbi Cymru

Welsh Rugby Union
Schweppes Cup Final

CARDIFF

versus

NEWPORT

Cardiff Arms Park
Saturday 26th April 1986

Ray Williams
Secretary W.R.U

Official Programme 50p

An exciting final saw Cardiff gain revenge for 1977 by winning 28-21. The teams lined up as shown here and it is worth noting that Rhys Morgan was making his third appearance for Newport in the final, being the only player to do so.

Undeb Rygbi Cymru
Welsh Rugby Union

Match Officials
Referee:
K. Rowlands (Ynysybwl)
Touch Judges:
C. Norling (Swansea)
W.D. Bevan (Swansea)

	Cardiff	**Newport**
	Cambridge Blue and Black	Black and Amber
Full Back (Cefnwr)	15 M. Rayer	15 R. Knight
Right wing (Asgell dde)	14 G. Cordle	14 M. Batten
Right Centre (Canolwr)	13 A.J. Donovan †	13 D. Pitt
Left Centre (Canolwr)	12 M. Ring †	12 P. Daniel
Left Wing (Asgell chwith)	11 A.M. Hadley †	11 J. White
Stand-off (Maswr)	10 W.G. Davies †	10 P. Turner
Scrum-half (Mewnwr)	9 N. O'Brien	9 N. Callard
Loose-head prop (Y rheng flaen)	1 J. Whitefoot †	1 J. Rawlins
Hooker (Bachwr)	2 A.J. Phillips (Captain) †	2 M.J. Watkins (Captain) †
Tight-head prop (Y rheng flaen)	3 I. Eidman †	3 R. Morgan †
Lock (Yr ail reng)	4 K. Edwards	4 J. Widdecombe
Lock (Yr ail reng)	5 R.L. Norster †	5 A. Perry
Left flanker (Blaenasgell)	6 O. Golding	6 R. Collins
No. 8 (Y rheng ol)	8 J.P. Scott †	8 D. Waters †
Right flanker (Blaenasgell)	7 G.J. Roberts †	7 R. Powell

Replacements	Replacements
16 P.M. Rees	16 S. McWilliams
17 D. Evans	17 D. Kirby
18 D. Gibbon	18 R. Stewart/A. Coombs
19 J. Souto	19 H. Ali
20 C. Collins	20 F. Hillman
21 R. Lakin	21 W. Randall

Kick-Off 3.00pm

† International

Phil May, last season's captain of Llanelli, shows the Schweppes Cup to supporters after receiving it at the presentation ceremony at the National Ground, Cardiff. Llanelli defeated Cardiff 15-14.

Newport played New Zealand on 31 October 1989 for almost certainly the last time. In 7 previous meetings Newport had never failed to provide opposition that the tourists could take lightly. Although 1963 was the club's only victory, all the other matches had been keenly contested. In 1989, however, Newport were a side struggling to find form and the All Blacks were world beaters. Winners of the inaugural Rugby World Cup in 1987, they were now fitter, faster and more 'professional' than ever before, though it was a further six years before they became professional in the financial sense of the word. Newport started badly even before a ball had been kicked. The traditional Maori Haka is usually faced up to but on this occasion Newport retreated under the posts only for Wayne Shelford to take his team up field and perform the ritual a matter of yards away from the home side. A deluge of points in the shape of 10 tries and 7 conversions meant that Newport were blown away 54-9. The pack, which was led by Shelford, featured a young Zinzan Brooke and hooking was Warren Gatland – now coach to the Irish national side.

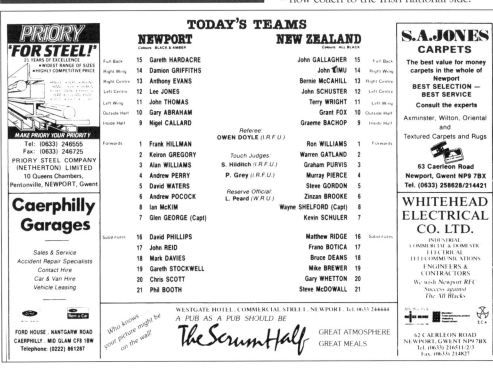

New Zealand captain Wayne Shelford received a stern warning from match referee Owen Doyle after punching Newport back row forward Andy Pocock, who lost four teeth from the blow. The crowd felt the offence warranted sending off, but Shelford got away with a caution. 'Buck' Shelford was New Zealand's most successful captain. Under his leadership 14 Tests were played, of which 13 were won with 1 match drawn. In addition, all 20 provincial matches played were won: 33 victories and a single draw is a record that will be difficult to beat. His powerful interpretation of the Maori Haka was magnificent and he must have relished the unusual circumstances in which this was performed at Newport.

A glance at the match programme shows Shelford joined in the back row by Zinzan Brooke playing on the blind side of the scrum. Brooke would duly take over at number eight from Shelford and become a New Zealand rugby legend. Zinny played exactly 100 matches for New Zealand, including 58 Tests. He scored a world record 17 tries by a forward in international rugby and added 3 drop goals to his tally of points. Adjectives abound when it comes to sporting achievement, but it's wise to listen when Bill McLaren describes Brooke as 'the best loose forward I've seen' and ex-All Black coach John Hart confirms 'there will never be another player like him'. It would be a further ten years before another truly great player from the southern hemisphere would take the stage at Rodney Parade.

More All Black action at Rodney Parade, this time the Welsh version – Neath RFC. Mark Jones, with ball in hand, and Rowland Hill break off the scrum in 1988. Glen George followed by Roger Powell break to cover the danger.

The 1990/91 season finally saw a league structure introduced in Wales. On two previous occasions, in 1908 and 1975, proposals for a league had been rejected by the clubs but at the third time of asking leagues were established under the sponsorship of Heineken. Newport played its first league fixture away at Maesteg on 22 September 1990.

When the league was finalised Newport found themselves as one of eight sides in Division One. A Premier League of ten sides had been formed from which it was decided that two clubs would be relegated at the end of the season, replaced by the top two clubs in Division One. The Newport players knew what was required of them and set about the task of securing promotion at the first attempt. They would not be denied. Declared champions with one match still remaining, the team only lost once, at home to Maesteg, who also went on to gain promotion. Ironically, the leagues were renamed for the following season, with Newport again finding themselves in Division One. Over the next eight seasons Newport struggled to consolidate their place in the top division. Season 1997/98 must be regarded as an all-time low for the club. All 14 matches were lost and to add insult to injury Newport also had two points deducted after being unable to fulfil the away fixture at Cardiff. The game had to be postponed as Newport were unable to find a front row. The two-point deduction effectively left Newport with minus two points for the season's total! It will be recalled that Newport and Cardiff used to meet four times a season with Newport never managing to win all four games. Cardiff did this on four occasions but never before, and hopefully never again, will Newport lose five games in a season to the same club. Caerphilly achieved this incredible statistic in 1998/99 by winning four league matches and a fixture in the European Shield. This picture shows happier days as Glen George and the team celebrate winning the Division One Championship in 1990/91.

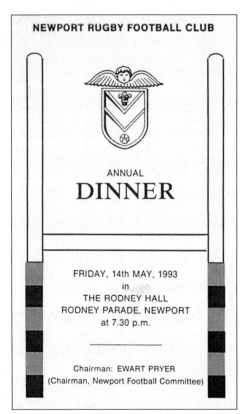

NEWPORT RUGBY FOOTBALL CLUB

ANNUAL

DINNER

FRIDAY, 14th MAY, 1993
in
THE RODNEY HALL
RODNEY PARADE, NEWPORT
at 7.30 p.m.

Chairman: EWART PRYER
(Chairman, Newport Football Committee)

The end of season annual dinner saw the presentation of the club awards to players, including trophies, badges and blazers. In addition to the players, club officials and administrators were invited as a thank you for all their contributions and help during the season.

Newport Rugby Football Club

Annual Rugby Dinner

*to be held in the Rodney Hall
on Friday 14th May, 1993
at 7pm for 7.30pm
Guest Speaker Mike Burton*

Gloucester   Barbarians   England   British Lions

Dress: Lounge Suit or Blazer

The 1992/93 First XV squad included, from left to right, back row: M. Roderick, J. Westwood, M. Sibthorpe, M. Yendle, D. Rees, B. McCracken, I. Jones, A. Dibble. Third row: A. Evans (physiotherapist), P. Ward (administrator), J. Williams, A. Carter, B. Watkins, K. Moseley, A. Allen, D. Waters, K. Withey, K. Westwood (coach), R. Powell (senior coach). Second row: A. Peacock, M. Davies, C. Black (hon. secretary), R. Bidgood, E. Pryer (chairman), Glen George (captain), D. Watkins (manager), K. Orrell, K. Lee. Front row: S. Duggan, I. Jeffries, C. Scott, D. Llewellyn. In its first 100 years, 121 players had represented Newport RFC in the Welsh team. As the club is older than the Welsh Rugby Union and there were breaks in play due to the two world wars the selection period was effectively reduced to 86 years. Consider then the 25-year period since the centenary and it is disappointing to record that only 19 players have been capped since 1975. It is surprising that seven of these players should appear in this team photograph: A. Carter, K. Moseley, D. Waters, M. Davis, R. Bidgood, G. George and D. Llewellyn had, or would, play for Wales while Andy Allen won 3 caps in 1990 when he was a Newbridge player.

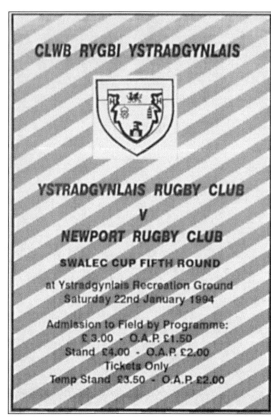

CLWB RYGBI YSTRADGYNLAIS

YSTRADGYNLAIS RUGBY CLUB

v

NEWPORT RUGBY CLUB

SWALEC CUP FIFTH ROUND

at Ystradgynlais Recreation Ground
Saturday 22nd January 1994

Admission to Field by Programme:
£3.00 - O.A.P. £1.50
Stand £4.00 - O.A.P. £2.00
Tickets Only
Temp Stand £3.50 - O.A.P. £2.00

One of those days you would rather forget: 22 January 1994, the fifth round of the SWALEC Cup and an away tie at Ystradgynlais. Left wing Ian Michael scored the try, Mike Lewis converted and added a penalty with Jason Williams kicking three penalties in reply. Ystradgynlais 10 Newport 9 – enough said.

MATCH BALL SPONSOR				

SATURDAY 22nd JANUARY 1994
at the Welfare Ground Ystradgynlais
Kick off 2.30 pm

MATCH BALL SPONSOR

B.G. ROBERTS WHOLESALE

TELEPHONE:
(0639) 845417

SWALEC CUP

YSTRADGYNLAIS R.F.C
WELSH CUP MATCHES
A GREAT TRADITION

	YSTRADGYNLAIS	NEWPORT	
15	Julian Hopkins	David Rees	15
14	Kerry Jones	Mike Puddy	14
13	Adrian Williams (Capt)	Roger Bidgood (Capt)	13
12	Celan Hopkins	Mark Yendle	12
11	Ian Micheal	Duncan Hughes	11
10	Mike Lewis	Jason Williams	10
9	Steffan Jenkins	Mark Roderick	9
1	Mark Harris	Andrew Dibble	1
2	Martin Thomas	Andrew Peacock	2
3	Andrew Howells	James Alvis	3
4	Russ Mcdonald	Mike Voyle	4
5	Nick Mabbitt	Chris Wyatt	5
6	John Morgan	Alan Carter	6
7	Geraint Thomas	Ben Watkins	7
8	Jim Jenkins	Richard Goodey	8

REPLACEMENTS
Ryan Woodley, Darrel Jones,
Steve McKay, David Love,
Damien Clancy, Bleddyn Howells

REPLACEMENTS
16. Anthony Evans 17. David Llewelyn
18. Chris Morris 19. Ian Jones
20. Ben Atkins 21. Chris Scott

Date	Teams	Results / Captains
1974	v Cardiff (H)	Lost 0 - 11 D.Isaac
1978	v Llanelli (H) (Lost on Try count)	Drew 6 - 6 K. Edwards
1981	v Swansea (H)	Lost 0 - 3 K. Edwards
1982	v Ebbw Vale (A)	Lost 9 - 18 A. Buchanan
1983	v Bridgend (H)	Lost 9 - 19 K. Edwads
1987	v Cardiff (H)	Lost 9 - 12 O. Jones
1994	v Newport (H)	? A. Williams

TOUCH JUDGE:	REFEREE:	TOUCH JUDGE:
Mr PHILLIP WILLIAMS	Mr JOHN GROVES	Mr NEIL FLOWERS

MATCH SPONSORS:

SWANSEA TRUCK CENTRE	ROOM 2000	BRIAN D. THOMAS INSURANCE SERVICES	CONTINENTAL SERVICE STATION

While still a student at Oxford University, Gareth Rees made his Newport debut against Maesteg on 12 February 1994. A prodigious goal kicker, he quickly started rattling up points and in 1995/96 he scored 386 points, breaking the club record of 368 previously held by Paul Turner. His 33 points against Abertillery in the same season is also a club record. Capped over 50 times by Canada, Rees has the distinction of having played in all four Rugby World Cup competitions. In 1995 Rees and future Newport player Rod Snow, together with South African James Dalton, were sent off. Both received thirty-day bans with Dalton being similarly punished and thereby missing the rest of South Africa's triumphant tournament. In 1999 Rees had his international swansong in the group matches and enjoyed a 100 per cent kicking success with 19 goals from 19 attempts. Perhaps his greatest day in a Canadian jersey was in Cardiff in November 1993. He scored 16 points and helped defeat Wales 26-24 with a performance that also earned him the Man of the Match award. Since leaving Newport, Gareth Rees has played his rugby in England at Wasps, Bedford and Harlequins, helping Wasps win the Courage League Championship in 1996/97 and the Tetley Cup in 1999.

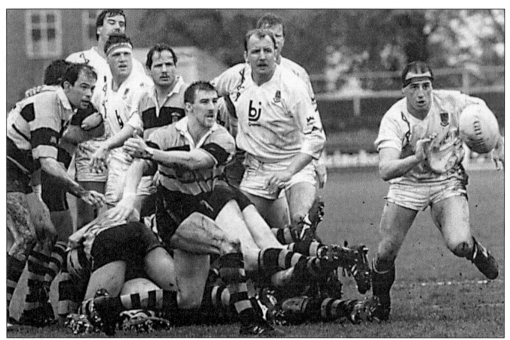

David Llewellyn playing at St Helens, Swansea, during his first spell with Newport. Llewellyn's career blossomed at Newport before he left to pursue his rugby career at Neath and then Ebbw Vale. While at Ebbw Vale he broke into the Welsh squad and was capped as a replacement on the 1998 tour to South Africa. In 1999 he returned to Newport after the Rugby World Cup, but his season was cut short by injury.

Like David Llewellyn, Ian Gough was first capped on the ill-fated tour to South Africa in 1998. The massive 13-96 Welsh defeat was no way to start your international career and Gough had to play the whole game while Llewellyn was a late replacement. Ian Gough moved to Pontypridd for the 1998/99 and 1999/2000 seasons but returned to Newport for the following season. Great things are expected of this young second row forward and his career will be followed with interest.

TODAY'S MATCH SPONSOR
HAZELLS HAULAGE

NEWPORT					ABERAVON
Colours: BLACK & AMBER					Colours: RED & BLACK HOOPS
Mark YENDLE	Cefnwr	15	Full Back		Don DAVIES
Richard REES	Asgell Dde	14	Right Wing		Barry GRABHAM
Duncan HUGHES	Canolwr Dde	13	Right Centre		Colin LAITY
Shane WEBLEY	Canolwr Chwith	12	Left Centre		Geraint WILLIAMS
Paul HOPKINS	Asgell Chwith	11	Left Wing		Simon HUTCHINSON
Gareth REES	Maswr	10	Stand-off		Mark WATTS
Jason HEWLETT	Mewnwr	9	Scrum-half		Gareth JOHN
Damon THOMAS	Prop Rhydd	1	Prop		Rob PRICE
Andrew PEACOCK	Bachwr	2	Hooker		Lloyd GILBY
Sean DUGGAN	Prop Tyn	3	Prop		Dai AUSTIN
Neil JONES	Clo	4	Lock		Simon THOMAS
Kevin MOSELEY	Clo	5	Lock		Paul MATTHEWS
Mark WORKMAN	Blaenasgellwr	6	Flanker		Billy SHENTON (Capt.)
Richard GOODEY (Capt.)	Wythwr	8	No. 8		Richard MORRIS
David GRAY	Blaenasgellwr	7	Flanker		Chris KINSEY
Andy ARENTSEN	Eilyddion		Replacements		Nick STORK
Martin JONES					Richard DIPLOCK
Mark RODERICK					Ian EVANS
Ian JONES					Paul CLAPHAM
Mark GORK-ROGERS					Justin HUGHES
Alun CARTER					Graham EVANS

REFEREE/DYFARNWR: CLAYTON THOMAS
TOUCH JUDGES/LLINANWYR: 1—H.J. WILSON 2—GLENN LEWIS
Newport RFC wish to thank today's Ball Sponsors:
JAMES GILBERT LTD · WILLIAM HILL ORGANISATION

In August 1995, after a meeting in Paris, the International Rugby Board announced the game would go open with immediate effect. Players could now earn money for their efforts. There had been great concern that, if the authorities had not acted, then control would be lost. There was a serious threat of outside parties forming professional teams on a worldwide basis to compete in a rugby circus. The 'shamateur' days were over, the threat of players lost to Rugby League would come to an end and everything would be fine. The only question now was where the money would come from to sustain a professional game. Any advantage would obviously lie with clubs that were currently successful. They would have a better chance of attracting sponsors, top class players and the public that would make the turnstiles click. Unfortunately, at this time, Newport were a struggling club and their leading players were tempted away. The first major casualty was Gareth Rees, whose departure to Wasps was one of several moves into English rugby by Welsh-based players. Newport would subsequently lose players to other Welsh clubs whose prospects were seen to be more favourable. In addition to Llewellyn and Gough, Chris Wyatt and Mike Voyle were lost to Llanelli and Richard Rees and Matthew Robinson joined Swansea. All these players subsequently became Welsh internationals. Without a large injection of capital there was no way the club would be able to compete at the highest level in the fast approaching new millennium. The above programme shows the Newport team selected to play Aberavon on 2 September 1995, the first game played by the club in the new professional era. Less than four years later, at the start of the 1999/2000 season, only David Gray of those listed above was to be found on the playing staff at Rodney Parade.

Newport Athletic Club

Telephones: OFFICE & GROUNDS 58193
SOCIAL CENTRE 67410

MEN

Member's Ticket

1962/63

THIS TICKET MUST BE
PRODUCED ON ALL OCCASIONS
WHEN ENTERING THE GROUNDS

NON-PLAYING

J. Watkins Esq.

NOT TRANSFERABLE

This Ticket expires on April 30th, 1963

708

FIRST XV—FIXTURES, 1962/63

1962
August
Sat. 25—Trials ... ... Home
September
Sat. 1—Penarth ... ... Home
„ 8—Bristol ... ... Home
„ 15—Neath ... ... Away
„ 22—Swansea ... ... Home
W. 26—Pontypool ... Away
Sat. 29—Llanelly ... ... Away
October
Sat. 6—Cardiff ... ... Away
W. 10—Crosskeys (F.L.) ... Home
Sat. 13—Blackheath ... Away
W. 17—Pontypool (F.L.) ... Home
Sat. 20—Gloucester ... Home
„ 27—Wasps ... ... Home
November
Sat. 3—Abertillery ... Away
„ 10—Cardiff ... ... Home
W. 14—Cambridge U. (F.L.) Home
Sat. 17—Leicester ... Home
„ 24—London Welsh ... Away
December
Sat. 1—Bristol ... ... Away
M. 10—Aberavon (F.L.) ... Home
Sat. 15—Harlequins ... Away
„ 22—Ebbw Vale ... Away
W. 26—Watsonians ... Home
Th. 27—U.A.U ... ... Home
Sat. 29—R.A.F. ... ... Home

A season ticket for the 1962/1963 season. The length of the season was quite rigidly maintained by the WRU, with no competitive rugby being played before 1 September and after 30 April. The ticket shows forty-seven fixtures for the season: all the leading clubs were played with four matches scheduled in an eight-day period over Christmas and six matches over eleven days in April. A much-reduced fixture list has seen the matches against the Universities Athletic Union, Oxford University and Cambridge University disappear together with the Services sides who were always popular visitors. Pontypridd, Dunvant and Caerphilly are now regularly played in the league structure at the expense of more traditional opponents such as Pontypool, Newbridge, Abertillery and Penarth. Cross-border competition is minimal, relying on European competition and the occasional friendly.

1963
January
Tue. 1—Watsonians ... Away
M. 7—Ebbw Vale (F.L.) ... Home
Sat. 12—Swansea ... ... Away
„ 19—Coventry ... ... Away
W. 23—Royal Navy (F.L.) Home
Sat. 26—Llanelly ... ... Home
February
Th. 7—Oxford University ... Home
Sat. 9—Leicester ... ... Away
„ 16—Cardiff ... ... Away
„ 23—Blackheath (F.L.) ... Home
March
Sat. 2—Cardiff ... ... Home
„ 9—Wasps ... ... Away
„ 16—Aberavon ... ... Away
W. 20—Penarth ... ... Away
Sat. 23—Gloucester ... ... Away
„ 30—Neath ... ... Home
April
Sat. 6—Bridgend ... ... Home
„ 13—Newbridge ... ... Home
M. 15—London Welsh ... Home
Tue. 16—Barbarians ... ... Home
Sat. 20—Plymouth ... ... Away
M. 22—Devonport Services Away
Tue. 23—Exeter ... ... Away
Sat. 27—Welsh Sevens Cardiff

HOME RUGBY INTERNATIONALS

Jan. 19th, 1963—Wales v. England
Feb. 23rd, 1963—England v. France
Mar. 9th, 1963—Wales v. Ireland
Mar. 16th, 1963—England v. Scotland

**THIS TICKET IS ISSUED SUBJECT
TO THE FOLLOWING CONDITIONS**

1. It is NOT TRANSFERABLE and will be forfeited if presented by any other than the person to whom it is issued and whose name is written thereon.

2. The Owner MUST when requested, produce it at the gate on entering the Ground, otherwise admittance may be refused unless the charge for admission is paid.

3. It admits the Owner to all Club Sports and Matches, except on such special occasions as the Committee shall decide (International, Trial and Charity Matches also excepted) during the Season 1962/63.

4. A Member is responsible for payment of his or her subscription until written notice of resignation is received by the Secretary.

5. No Member whose subscription shall not have been paid within 7 days from the date upon which it is due, shall be allowed the privileges of the Club until such subscription shall be paid.

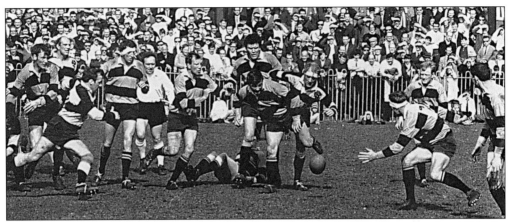

One major casualty of the modern era is the fixture with the Barbarians. First played in 1893, the Barbarians were regular visitors to Rodney Parade. Newport, along with Penarth, Cardiff and Swansea, made up the opposition on the Easter tour of South Wales and the crowds flocked to watch the invitation side and the exciting rugby they always produced. This photograph was taken on Bank Holiday Tuesday, April 1969. The Barbarians won this game 16-3, one of Newport's four defeats in the Championship season. Del Haines reaches for the loose ball, watched by John Jeffery, Jeff Watkins, Paul Watts and Vic Perrins. Treharne and Britton are ready to support.

In 1982 Newport's fixture with the Barbarians was moved to a midweek slot at the start of the season, where it remained for fifteen years. The last game was played in 1996, when the Barbarians recorded their biggest victory over Newport by winning 86-33. By then fixtures with Penarth (1986) and Swansea (1994) had been laid to rest and the Cardiff match scheduled for Easter 1996 had been cancelled. The cartoon shown here, which was produced in Newport's centenary year, pales into insignificance when compared to later results.

When the Newport-Barbarians fixture ended in 1996 the clubs had met on 90 occasions. Newport had won 51 games, the Barbarians 35 and 4 games were drawn. The Barbarians were founded in 1890 and in due course France and the southern hemisphere countries established their own versions of the famous club. In 1979 the Home Unions Committee invited the South African Barbarians to tour the UK. A multi-racial touring party was selected comprising of twenty-four players – eight white, eight coloured and eight black. The tour went ahead although, as expected, it met with opposition from many quarters. The side were a great success and in the final match of the tour played at Rodney Parade. Newport won an exciting game 21-15, probably the best result in a miserable season for the club. The South African side included future Springboks Rob Louw, Divan Serfontein, Martiens Le Roux and Errol Tobias. While Serfontein would captain the 'Boks, it was his half-back partner Tobias, who became the first black player to be capped by the South African selectors when he played against Ireland in 1981. In this photograph Newport's Lynn Jones jumps for the ball while Louw (extreme left) and Serfontein (16) watch on.

Ken Jones

Bryn Meredith

Brian Price

In celebration of the WRU centenary in 1980/81 a set of fifty cigarette cards was commissioned. Drawn by local cartoonist 'Gren', the set contained eight players who had represented Newport. Depicting fifty all-time great Welsh internationals, the inclusion of the four players on this page could not be questioned. For the record, the other four were Arthur Gould, Teddy Morgan, Gwynn Nicholls and John Gwilliam.

David Watkins

Consider this – at the end of the twentieth century a player in a Division One side, regularly selected for first team duty, could expect to play 30 to 36 games a season: 22 in the league, a minimum of 6 in European competition and a further 6 in the Welsh Cup if the team reached the final. If the club maintained unprecedented success for ten years, the player escaped injury, stayed with the club and wasn't called up for international duties, he would play around 370 games. In its 125-year history, four players have played for Newport RFC on over 400 occasions. All great clubmen, they deserve particular recognition in these pages. Ian Ford was the first player to make 400 appearances for the club. By the time he retired in 1966 the figure had risen to 482 and it would not be until 1978 that Keith Poole would improve on it. After making his debut in 1949/50, Ian forged strong second row partnerships with John Herrera and then Brian Price. He gained 2 Welsh caps in 1959 against England and Scotland. In both games his second row partner was R.H. Williams of Llanelli. After retiring from the game Ian emigrated to New Zealand, where he was employed by the Department of Horticulture. He has since relocated in Wales and is frequently seen watching the fortunes of Newport at Rodney Parade.

Keith Poole played his 400th game for the club at Swansea on 28 September 1974, becoming the second player to reach this landmark. He went on to play a total of 486 games, with his last on the Canadian tour in May 1978. His first appearance was against Gloucester on 25 September 1963 and his second against New Zealand one month later. The twenty year old was drafted into the side when injury forced Brian Cresswell to withdraw. Keith played against the three major tourists, never finishing on the losing side, and won a Cup Winners' medal in 1977.

A product of Newport Youth, Rhys Morgan made his First XV debut in 1973. A powerful tighthead prop, he served the club with great distinction until retiring in 1990. He became the first player to make 500 appearances for the club, finishing his career with a total of 538. Morgan broke Keith Poole's record number of appearances during his season as club captain in 1987/88. Called up as a late replacement, he won a Welsh cap against Scotland in 1984.

The fourth, and probably last, Newport player to make over 400 appearances for the club was second row David 'Muddy' Waters. From his debut in 1973 to his last appearance in 1996, David Waters played a massive 701 games. This record will surely never be beaten: twenty seasons at thirty-five games a season is not likely in the modern era. David also holds another record for the club that will be difficult to beat. On the 1979 tour to South Africa he was sent off twice in the space of nine days. He won 4 caps in 1986, although he had been selected twice the previous season in place of the injured Robert Norster. On both occasions the matches were postponed due to bad weather and Norster returned when play was resumed. Player profiles have been regular features in match programmes for many years. David Waters was featured in the Newport-Bridgend programme on 12 April 1976. The details included his favourite food – curry – and favourite drink – beer. A total of 701 games for Newport on a diet of curry and beer and still turning out for Merthyr at forty-five years of age is quite an achievement.

Six
Brown, Black and
Amber

As the 1990s drew to a close Newport RFC had to accept that the period reflected the worst decade in its history. One could be forgiven for believing that the advent of leagues and then professionalism had been some sort of conspiracy against the club. If these events had taken place in any other decade in its history the club would have coped but in the 1990s Newport began a downward spiral that appeared to be out of control. Lack of success led to little interest from the paying public, which failed to generate the necessary revenue to bring the leading players to Rodney Parade. Without a quality playing staff the spiral could not be reversed. A group of local businessmen had supported the club through this period and their backing ensured that the financial side of the equation didn't get out of control. In 1989, Bisley Office Furniture had opened a factory in Newport. The company had been established in the Home Counties by Tony Brown some twenty years earlier. He soon became interested in the fortunes of Newport RFC and became a vice-president. In 1998, Newport Athletic Club were incorporated, with Tony Brown taking his place on a high profile board of directors. The following year he made a huge commitment to the club, agreeing to underwrite it for three years. With this enormous backing Newport could now start to look for the players that would restore it to its rightful place in Welsh rugby.

In 1998 the Welsh Rugby Union appointed New Zealander Graham Henry as coach to the national team. He took no time in searching out players who had not featured in the international plans of his predecessors and one such find was prop forward Peter Rogers. During a period in South Africa, Rogers had played provincial rugby for Transvaal and appeared in the Super 12 competition for Gauteng Falcons. The first of his 17 Welsh caps to date was won against France in 1999 while he was playing for London Irish. When he won his fourth cap against Argentina in Buenos Aries he was a Newport player. Peter Rogers was the first major signing by the club on its summer spending spree. In this photograph he is seen helping to bring Llanelli's Rupert Moon to a halt.

While the club was actively seeking new players in the summer of 1999 it was essential that a mix of quality and youth was retained from the existing squad. Canadian international prop forward Rod Snow had joined Newport in November 1995 and become a favourite with the faithful band of supporters. After experiencing the lows it was particularly pleasing that Rod stayed at Rodney Parade to play a part in the club's exciting future. His international career began in 1995 when he was chosen as hooker against Argentina. Some 30 caps later and with 2 Rugby World Cups under his belt Rod Snow is one of those larger than life characters known throughout the rugby world.

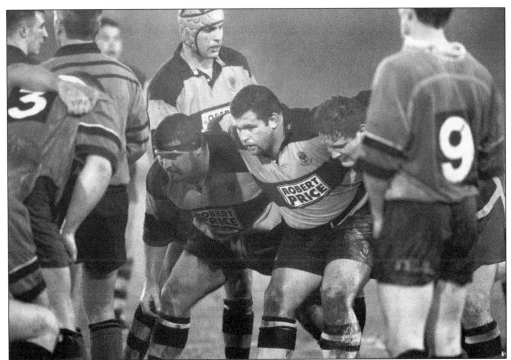

Above: Australian Damien Cummins was a regular in the Newport front row during the 1999/2000 season. In total he appeared in 29 of the 32 matches played. In this photograph, the front row of Snow, Cummins and Rogers gets ready to lock horns with the opposition in the WRU Challenge Cup match against Cardiff. Snow scored Newport's only try in a thrilling 22-13 victory over the old enemy. This was one of many highlights during the season.
Right: Now recognised as part of the hooker's work, Damien Cummins throws the ball into a line-out. This has become an important aspect of the game with line-out possession almost being taken for granted by the side with the put in.

During the summer of 1999 Newport were not alone in their recruitment drive. Cardiff signed Neil Jenkins, Craig Quinnell and Martin Williams and, further west, Llanelli were joined by Dafydd James and Newport's Matt Cardey. Cardey's departure had left the club seeking a new full-back. Although Gareth Cull and Justin Thomas both joined Newport, it was the signing of current Welsh full-back Shane Howarth that stole the headlines. Cardiff believed they had their man only to see Tony Brown close the deal with Howarth in record time. Seen here on the burst, Howarth reverted to the outside-half position in the latter part of the season.

It was announced in August that Shane Howarth would be club captain for the coming season. However, his World Cup commitments with Wales prevented him from making his first appearance until the away game against Glasgow on 5 November when he played in the centre. In his second game at Dunvant he scored 26 points, including 2 tries. Howarth took over the place kicking duties for the rest of the season and in his 21 appearances scored a total of 288 points.

Season 1995/96 saw the introduction of a European Cup competition, with just twelve sides competing for a trophy eventually won by Toulouse. Although English clubs had not entered, the tournament was seen to be successful enough to continue and a secondary competition, the European Conference, was introduced the following season. In 1996/97 forty-four European clubs competed in the two competitions and Newport were involved in Pool A of the four-pool European Conference. The team's first match in the tournament was away at Agen but the first home game saw Newport entertain Newbridge who had all of fifteen miles to travel.

Although Newport RFC competed in the European Conference (renamed European Shield in 1998) in four successive seasons, they failed to progress beyond the initial group stages. Of 23 matches played in the competitions 9 were won with 14 lost. The progress made by the club in 1999/2000 means that they will compete in the premier competition in 2000/01. The European Cup has become the major tournament in the northern hemisphere and for any club taking part the financial opportunities that success guarantees are huge.

South Africa and its rugby has long been associated with Newport RFC, with the friendship between the club and the country having developed over 100 years of competition. It was therefore fitting that Newport completed the signing of Gary Teichmann in August 1999. The media in both countries had been speculating on the possible move and when Teichmann visited Newport on a flying twenty-four-hour visit the rumours were rife. Impressed with what he saw, on his return to South Africa it was a matter of days before he made the announcement that he would be joining Newport on a two-year contract.

Gary Teichmann began his rugby career with College Rovers in Durban before joining Natal. He made a total of 144 appearances for Natal, 59 as captain, and led them to successive Currie Cup wins in 1995 and 1996. Teichmann made his international debut in South Africa's first game as World Champions, against Wales in Johannesburg, scoring a try in the Springboks' 40-11 victory. He went on to win a total of 42 caps, 33 as captain, which is a South African record. His total of 42 caps is also a record for a number eight and 39 consecutive appearances is another record for his country. He also captained South Africa in every match of their record-equalling 17 consecutive Test victories. Gary's last appearance for South Africa was against New Zealand in the 1999 Tri-nations series. There was great controversy in South Africa when he was omitted from the World Cup squad and this rages on twelve months later as the Springboks fail to live up to expectations. However, South Africa's loss is Newport's gain and since joining the Rodney Parade club his influence both on and off the field has been enormous. When Shane Howarth decided to relinquish the club captaincy it was in the knowledge that in Gary Teichmann there was a player who could step into the position with ease. A natural leader, Teichmann guided the club through the last months of the season to the best finish since their arrival in the top division. In this photograph Teichmann leads the team out behind the match mascot for Newport's last match of the season against Dunvant.

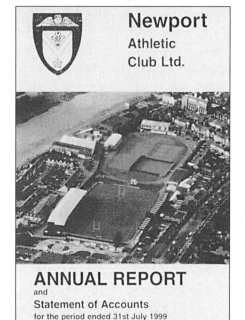

Newport
Athletic
Club Ltd.

ANNUAL REPORT
and
Statement of Accounts
for the period ended 31st July 1999
and
Notice of Annual General Meeting

Season 1998 saw the incorporation of Newport Athletic Club Ltd. The audited accounts showed a net asset value of £983,567, which was distributed among the club membership, with each member receiving an allocation of 936 Ordinary Shares at £1. At the first annual general meeting of the company, held at Rodney Parade on 18 May 2000, a resolution was passed to change the name of the company to Newport Rugby Football Club Limited.

Certificate Number	Bargain Number	Firm Code	Transfer Number	Registration Date	Number of Shares
A00350-H				09-OCT-98	*936*

NEWPORT ATHLETIC CLUB LIMITED

Incorporated in England and Wales under the Companies Act 1985
Registered No. 3559359

Ordinary Shares

This is to certify that

A455

S LEWIS
13 BASSALEG ROAD
NEWPORT
S WALES NP9 3EB

00000003510

is/are the registered holder(s) of

NINE HUNDRED AND THIRTY SIX

fully paid Ordinary Shares of £1·00 each in **NEWPORT ATHLETIC CLUB LIMITED**, subject to the Memorandum and Articles of Association of the Company.

Christopher J. Hill
Director and Company Secretary

David Watkins
Chairman

Given under the Seal of the Company at the registration date shown above.

Note:

No transfer of the above-mentioned shares or any portion thereof will be registered unless this certificate has been deposited at the offices of Exchange Registrars Limited, 18 Park Place, Cardiff, CF1 3PD.

114

Newport RFC has always had a strong youth XV. In 1998 the club won the Welsh Youth Cup and it is good to see players from the side making their mark in the senior team. Back row forward Alix Popham is a well-seasoned player at just twenty years of age. He has played for the Welsh Youth XV and was a member of the Grand Slam-winning Wales Under-21 side in 1998/99. He captained the side in the following season and was called into the Welsh senior squad as a replacement for the match against Scotland. On the Welsh development tour to Canada in 2000, Popham led the side in three out of five matches, all of which were won.

Another product of Newport youth rugby, Matthew J. Watkins is a centre with huge promise. Like Popham he featured in the Welsh Under-21 XV in 1998/99 and was also capped at youth level. He was a member of the Welsh squad that toured Argentina in 1999 and was a replacement on two occasions. Popham and Watkins are still to be capped at senior level but both players are knocking on the door and it can only be a matter of time before their ambitions are realised.

In a game that was decided by the last kick, Newport defeated Swansea at Rodney Parade 23-21. This photograph shows outside-half Franco Smith stepping inside the Swansea defence. Smith was another of Newport's South African imports. His 9 caps included 2 appearances against Wales, both in 1998. He played in the 96-13 victory in Pretoria and at Wembley when South Africa won a closer match 28-20. Franco played a total of 23 matches for Newport before returning to South Africa at the end of the season to pursue his international ambitions.

In the professional era, movement between the Union and League codes of rugby has become a two-way process. Previously, if a player had signed to play Rugby League his Union days were over but all that changed in 1995. Andy Marinos, a Zimbabwean by birth, played Union for Natal before joining Australian Rugby League side Sydney Bulldogs. He returned to South Africa, picking up his Union career with Western Province and making 13 appearances for the Super 12 side Western Stormers. Eligible for Wales, Marinos appeared in the uncapped game against the USA in the build-up to the World Cup.

One could be forgiven for assuming that with all the star players that Newport had at their disposal success would come easily. This, of course, was unrealistic. The players needed time to gel and there would be disappointment to overcome, particularly in the first half of the season. The European Shield campaign never got off the ground. The first two games at Bedford and at home to Castres were both lost and Newport's chances of progressing beyond the group stages looked slim. Although three games were won, the defeat away to Castres ensured the club would take no further part in the competition. The run in the WRU Challenge Cup ended with a disappointing performance at Llanelli but it was in the league that Newport had its highest hopes as a top four finish would guarantee a place in the European Cup in the following season. At the end of February, with 14 matches played, 8 wins and a drawn game away to Glasgow had left Newport with 7 matches to play and plenty to do. Away defeats at Pontypridd and Ebbw Vale had raised huge question marks and even the international players in the side did not escape the flak from the terraces. The pressures of international rugby had prompted Shane Howarth to resign as club captain and the politics of the game would put this most dedicated clubman under further stress. With Teichmann now leading the team, the last 7 matches were approached with everybody knowing what was required. All 7 games were won and the club ended the campaign in style. The supporters had returned to Rodney Parade and, as can be seen in this photograph, there was plenty to cheer.

One player who certainly knew what it was like to be caught up in the politics of rugby was Jason Jones-Hughes. He became the victim of a dispute between the Welsh Rugby Union and its Australian counterpart. Jones-Hughes had played for the Australian Barbarians and the view down under was that in so doing he had committed himself to an international future with the Wallabies. When the situation was resolved Jones-Hughes was allowed to take his place in the Welsh squad preparing for the World Cup. The loser in this was Andy Marinos who had been on standby for Wales and had to step down.

Newport had four class centres to call upon. In addition to Jones-Hughes and Marinos, Matthew J. Watkins and Jonathan Pritchard were competing for the positions. The senior pairing of Jones-Hughes and Marinos were in pole position at the end of the season having started 9 of the last 10 games. However, don't expect them to have it all their own way in 2000/01.

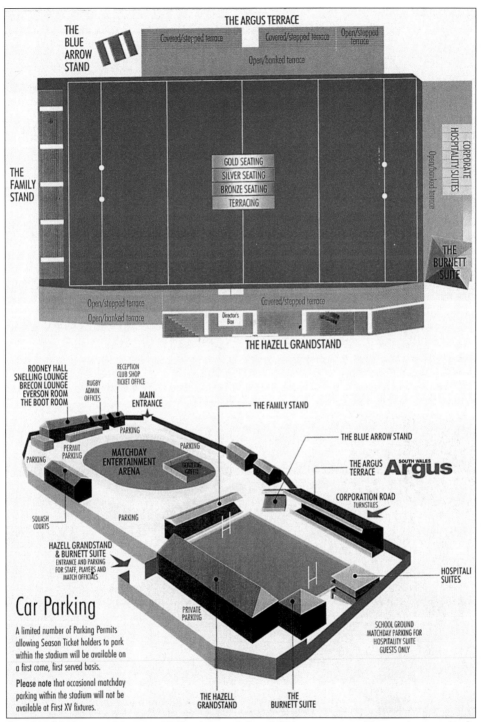

THE ARGUS TERRACE

THE BLUE ARROW STAND

Covered/stepped terrace   Covered/stepped terrace   Open/stepped terrace

Open/banked terrace

THE FAMILY STAND

GOLD SEATING
SILVER SEATING
BRONZE SEATING
TERRACING

CORPORATE HOSPITALITY SUITES

Open/banked terrace

THE BURNETT SUITE

Open/stepped terrace
Open/banked terrace

Covered/stepped terrace

Director's Box

THE HAZELL GRANDSTAND

RODNEY HALL
SNELLING LOUNGE
BRECON LOUNGE
EVERSON ROOM
THE BOOT ROOM

RUGBY ADMIN. OFFICES

RECEPTION
CLUB SHOP
TICKET OFFICE

MAIN ENTRANCE

THE FAMILY STAND

PARKING

PERMIT PARKING

PARKING

MATCHDAY ENTERTAINMENT ARENA

PARKING

BOWLING GREEN

THE BLUE ARROW STAND

THE ARGUS TERRACE   SOUTH WALES **Argus**

CORPORATION ROAD
TURNSTILES

SQUASH COURTS

PARKING

HAZELL GRANDSTAND & BURNETT SUITE
ENTRANCE AND PARKING FOR STAFF, PLAYERS AND MATCH OFFICIALS

HOSPITALI SUITES

Car Parking

A limited number of Parking Permits allowing Season Ticket holders to park within the stadium will be available on a first come, first served basis.

Please note that occasional matchday parking within the stadium will not be available at First XV fixtures.

PRIVATE PARKING

SCHOOL GROUND
MATCHDAY PARKING FOR HOSPITALITY SUITE GUESTS ONLY

THE HAZELL GRANDSTAND

THE BURNETT SUITE

In the 1999/2000 season Newport RFC celebrated their 125th anniversary. During this time Rodney Parade has not changed a great deal but the above plans show that exciting new developments are on the way. Extra seating and hospitality areas at the ground together with a complete refurbishment of the clubhouse will ensure that all spectators enjoy rugby at Rodney Parade.

Returning to Newport in 1999, David Llewellyn had a season of mixed fortune. A member of Wales' World Cup squad he made an appearance as a replacement in the group game against Japan. He lost his place in the Welsh squad for the Six Nations and an injury received against Swansea brought his season to a premature end. Here, Llewellyn cleans up while Cardiff players Tait, Voyle, Jenkins and Moore look on.

With Llewellyn sidelined, Newport were fortunate to have Dale Burn to call upon for the remainder of the season. A favourite with the crowd, Burn took his chances well, including a four-try haul against Glasgow. Here, Dale Burn ends the season with another try, this time against Dunvant.

Left wing Ben Breeze joined Newport from Bristol in 1999. His 25 appearances in the season brought him 16 tries, making him the top try scorer in the Premier League. Caerphilly right wing Chris Batsford just hangs on to prevent Breeze scoring try number 17.

West Walian Allan Lewis became Director of Rugby at Rodney Parade in 1998. Also part of the current national management team, he has coached Wales at under-19, under-21 and 'A' levels. He leads a coaching team at Newport assisted by Ian Smith and Nigel Callard. Coaching is in many ways a thankless occupation: win and you're a hero, but lose and the knives are out. There are signs that Allan and his team are putting together a squad of players who are prepared to play an exciting brand of rugby that will get results.

While the team is reaching parts never reached before on the field – such as the Heineken European Cup – the off-the-field staff are trying to do the same: taking the game to the Newport public or bringing them to the game is of top priority. Attracting families to the ground proved very successful at the end of the season. Marquees, music and entertainment for children were all part of the package and they loved it! With the teams doing the business on the field, the bars did the business off it.

Even props can smile! Peter Rogers puts pen to paper and makes someone's day.

Since the game went open in 1995, Rugby Union has struggled to find its way. International stadiums are always full on the big occasions, but these events are very often misleading when trying to analyse the true popularity of the sport. At club level things are not quite so cut and dried. Huge expenses are now involved in running the game and words like cart and horse, chicken and egg, often spring to mind. One thing is certain – success on the field is paramount in the equation. The crowds will follow a winning team and it is essential that future generations are introduced to the game and in particular Newport Rugby Football Club. These photographs suggest progress is being made. Maybe some of these lads will be a part of Newport teams in the years to come.

Every club has one and every club needs one – the unsung hero: the player who probably won't play international rugby, won't steal the headlines but, most importantly, won't let the side down. Post-war years have seen the likes of Roger Powell, Jeff Watkins, Ian Barnard, Neville Johnson and John Widdecombe fall into this category. Of course there are many other names that could be added and, indeed, fill the next few pages. All readers will have their own favourite. What about Paul Watts and Del Haines? Take your pick. In recent seasons Richard Goodey, Ian Jones and Sven Cronk deserve mentioning and in the current team Gareth Taylor fits the bill. Not only does Taylor play his rugby in the top league but he is also a full-time police officer. There was nothing unusual in that in years gone by, but in the modern era it is almost unheard of. Newport played 32 games in season 1999/2000. Gareth Taylor started in 24 and was a replacement in a further 4 matches. In this photograph Taylor is where he and his kind should be – up on his team-mates' shoulders.

Englishmen, Irishmen, Scots, Kiwis, Aussies, South Africans, Canadians and a Czech have all played for Newport. Now a Fijian can be added to the list. Simon Raiwalui – all 6ft 6in and 19 stone of him – joined the club in 1999 and made his first appearance against Caerphilly in October. A second row forward and utility back, Simon is captain of the Fijian national team.

On 15 April 1989 the worst tragedy in British sporting history occurred. An FA Cup semi-final between Liverpool and Nottingham Forest was to be played at Hillsborough in Sheffield, but instead a total of 94 people lost their lives, crushed by the sheer volume of spectators allowed onto the terracing. In the aftermath new legislation introduced strict regulations aimed at spectator safety at all sporting venues. Eleven years later, over the weekend of 15 and 16 April, a one-minute silence was observed at all matches throughout the UK. Here, the Newport team pay their respects before the league match with Edinburgh.

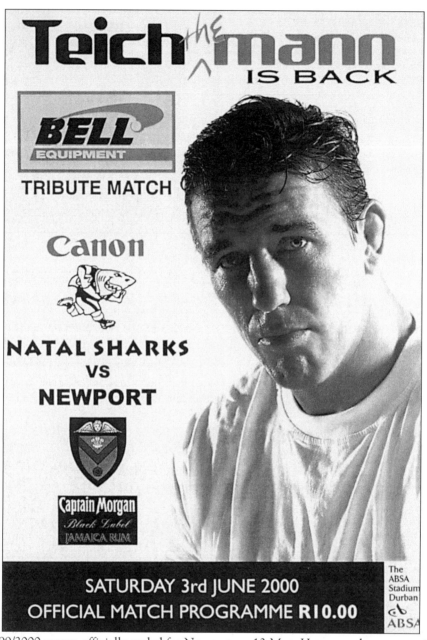

Teich*the*mann

IS BACK

BELL EQUIPMENT

TRIBUTE MATCH

Canon

NATAL SHARKS
VS
NEWPORT

Captain Morgan *Black Label* JAMAICA RUM

SATURDAY 3rd JUNE 2000
OFFICIAL MATCH PROGRAMME R10.00

The ABSA Stadium Durban

ABSA

The 1999/2000 season officially ended for Newport on 13 May. However, there were still two games to be played. The club had been invited to South Africa to take part in a match against Natal Sharks to be held in honour of Gary Teichmann. The tribute match was to be played on 3 June and a week earlier a game with Gary's first club, College Rovers, had also been arranged. A crowd of 4,000 supporters turned out to watch Newport gain a 21-13 victory over the Rovers and a week later at the newly named ABSA Stadium nearly 34,000 were present to salute Natal's favourite son. Although Newport were beaten 25-52, they took a lot of credit from the game. The occasion, perhaps more important than the rugby, saw some names from the not too distant past take the field in the latter stages of the game – Henry Honiball, James Small and Andre Joubert among others gave the Newport side plenty to think about.

The game was Newport's second appearance at the home of Natal rugby. During the tour in 1973 Newport had lost an entertaining game 7-20 at Kings Park as it was known then (and still is locally).

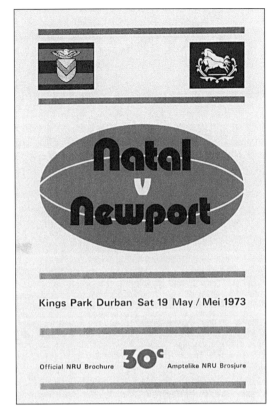

Natal v Newport

Kings Park Durban Sat 19 May / Mei 1973

Official NRU Brochure **30c** Amptelike NRU Brosjure

The players and officials were not on their own in Durban. The supporters' club had organised a tour and fifty-two of the Newport faithful made their presence felt. It wasn't that long ago that it was a struggle to get fifty supporters to travel to an away game in Wales!

Newport Rugby Football Club celebrated 125 years of rugby in 1999/2000. From great heights the club had also experienced great lows. The 1990s looked as if they would never end and where this great club would be in the new millennium was of major concern. Happily, it now looks as if the downward spiral has been checked and that the immediate future is in good hands, both on and off the field. This photograph shows the principal players in the last act of a 125-year-old play. From left to right, back row: Andy Marinos, David Gray, Alix Popham, Matthew J. Watkins, Jason Forster, Franco Smith, David Llewellyn. Third row: Mostyn Brown (attendant), Jim McCreedy (team manager), Phil Ward (team administrator), Mike Delahay (physiotherapist), Gareth Taylor, Joe Powell, Mark Workman, Paul Jones, Simon Raiwalui, Andy Gibbs, Damien Cummins, Mark Jones (head groundsman), Trystan Bevan (fitness co-ordinator), Nigel Callard (coach), Ian Smith (coach), Kevin Brown (attendant). Second row: Paul Young, Rod Snow, Martin Hazell (president), Jason Jones-Hughes, Tony Brown (chief executive), Gary Teichmann (captain), David Watkins (chairman), Shane Howarth, Allan Lewis (director of rugby), Ceri Jones, Peter Rogers. Front row: Dale Burn, Martyn Llewellyn, Scott Mitchell, Ben Breeze, Jon Pritchard, Neil McKim. James Gaunt, Justin Thomas. One last thought: it's ironic that in playing a game that only recently gave in to the power of money, Newport Rugby Club was formed because Thomas Phillips, an Englishman, brought his business to the town and it was given a lifeline as a consequence of Tony Brown, another Englishman, bringing his business to Newport.